GRAMMAR & DRILLBOOK

English as a Second Language

Helen Brennan Memorial Library

WILLARD D. SHEELER

English as a Second Language

Helen Brennan Memorial Library

This book is co-distributed in the United States of America by English Language Services, Inc. and Oxford University Press, Inc.

ENGLISH LANGUAGE SERVICES, INC.

Published by English Language Services, Inc.

Copyright © English Language Services, Inc. 1978
Philippines Copyright 1978
Taiwan Copyright 1978
Indonesia Copyright 1978
Korea Copyright 1978

Library of Congress Catalog Card Number 75-10596

All rights reserved. No part of this book may be reproduced or transmitted in any form or by any means, electronic or mechanical, including photocopying, recording or by any information storage and retrieval system, without permission in advance in writing from the publisher, English Language Services, Inc.

Printing   2   3   4   5   6   7   8   9   10

ISBN 0-89285-037-x

Printed in the United States of America

INTRODUCTION

In this book the learner of English finds a presentation of grammar of the language along with a great deal of practice material. The book is intended for students from the intermediate to low-advanced level. Generally speaking, the grammatical explanations are not too difficult for students of this level to understand by themselves. The practice material, of course, will serve as additional examples of many points. Some very elementary matters (such as noun inflection) are not discussed in detail but are taken for granted.

This volume discusses grammar in sixty-eight numbered points which focus on the general areas of (1) the make-up of the noun phrase (different kinds of nouns, modifiers of nouns, etc.), (2) indirect speech and (3) special complements of verbs having infinitives, gerunds, base-form verbs, indirect objects and object complements. These matters enable us to describe most of the common English sentence patterns.

Under each of the grammar points are explanations—phrased as simply as possible—and examples. There are often *Practices* embedded in the narrative sections of the grammar to give immediate practice on some mechanical aspect of the grammar point. *Exercises* for each grammar point are more challenging. As the student studies each grammar point he may either turn to its exercises at once or he may wait and go through all the exercises for that group of grammar points together. The exercises are grouped together in four Exercise Sections in the book.

Extra Drills

Throughout the book there are references to Extra Drills. These drills are printed in a separate book titled *Extra Drills and Practices*.

The *Grammar and Drillbook* can be used in many intermediate and lower advanced course programs. It is particularly appropriate with Books 5 and 6 of *Welcome to English,* which follows the grammar points in the same order—grammar points 1-34 in Book 5 and the remainder 35-68 in Book 6.

It is not essential to work through the *Grammar and Drillbook* starting from the beginning. The sections on Indirect Speech, for example, can be studied without reference to the preceding Noun Phrase sections. This feature makes the book particularly useful for grammar review and reference purposes.

The author expresses appreciation to the several teachers and students of the ELS Language Center in Washington, D.C. who tried out much of this text before publication, and also to Rayner W. Markley for his help in writing several sections of the grammar and exercises. Special thanks go to William E. Norris for his many helpful suggestions for improving several sections of the text.

TABLE OF CONTENTS

Introductory Unit	1-6
Noun Phrases	7-58
Section 1	7-14
1. Nouns	7
2. Count and Mass Nouns	8
3. Words Used as Both Count and Mass Nouns	9
4. Some Noun Modifiers	10
5. Noun Determiners	11
6. Articles and Demonstratives; *some, any, no*	11
7. Summary: Noun Phrases	14
Section 2	15-22
8. Noun Modifiers: Prepositional Phrases	15
9. Pronouns	16
10. Noun Determiners: *more* and *most; enough; plenty of*	17
11. Noun Determiners: *a lot of* and *lots of; much/many;*	
(a) little/(a) few; a great (good) deal of	19
12. Noun Substitutes	20
13. Summary: Noun Phrases	22
Section 3	23-32
14. Adjective Precedence	23
15. Noun Determiners: *some* and *any* with Strong Stress	24
16. Noun Determiners: *either/neither; another/other;*	
each and *every*	25
17. Indefinite Pronouns	30
18. Summary: Noun Phrases	32
Section 4	33-40
19. Noun Determiners: *all (the)* and *both (the)*	33
20. Predeterminers	35
21. Adjective + *one* or *ones*	37
22. Pre-Noun Modifiers (Summary)	38
23. Summary: Noun Phrases	38

v

Exercises for Sections 1-4   41-58

Direct and Indirect Speech   59-104
Section 5   59-67
    24. Sentences as Objects of Transitive Verbs   59
    25. Direct Speech   61
    26. Indirect Speech   62
    27. Indirect Speech: Verb Forms and Tenses   64
    28. Indirect Speech: Choice of Tenses   67

Section 6   68-74
    29. *Wh*-Question Words and Transformations   68
    30. Indirect Questions: *Wh*-Questions   72

Section 7   75-79
    31. Indirect Questions: Yes/No Questions   75
    32. Indirect Speech: with Imperatives   78

Section 8   80-85
    33. Indirect Speech: Pronoun Forms   80
    34. Indirect Speech: Adverbials of Time and Place;
        Verbs *come/go* and *bring/take*   82

Exercises for Sections 5-8   86-104

Infinitives and Gerunds;
Conjunctions and Compounding   105-128
Section 9   105-111
    35. Verb + Infinitive   105
    36. Special Verb Expressions   106
    37. Adjective + Infinitive   109
    38. Verb or Adjective + Infinitive: Short Answers   109
    39. Infinitive of Purpose   110

Section 10   112-118
    40. Verb + Gerund   112
    41. Preposition + Gerund   112
    42. Verbs Followed by Either Gerunds or Infinitives   115
    43. Gerunds and Infinitives as Subjects and Complements   116
    44. *It* and *there* as Sentence Subjects   116

Section 11 — 119-123
45. Nominal Phrases — 119
46. Noun Compounds — 120

Section 12 — 124-128
47. Compound Noun Phrases — 124
48. Conjunctions with Other Structures — 126
49. The Conjunction *but* — 127
50. Special Nouns in Reference to Number — 128

Exercises for Sections 9-12 — 129-140

Appositives, Participles; Indirect Objects and Other Complement Constructions — 141-184
Section 13 — 141-146
51. Adjectives Used as Nominals — 141
52. Appositives — 142
53. Infinitives and Gerunds with Different Meanings after Certain Verbs — 144
54. Compound Modifiers Using Numbers — 145
55. Noun Phrase + Infinitive — 145

Section 14 — 147-154
56. Participles as Noun Modifiers: *-ing* Form — 147
57. *-Ing* Forms as True Adjectives — 149
58. Participles as Noun Modifiers: *-ed* Form — 150
59. Contrast of *-ing* and *-ed* Forms — 153

Section 15 — 155-161
60. Verbs Followed by Two Objects: Indirect Object with *to* — 155
61. Verbs Followed by Two Objects: Indirect Object with *for* — 156
62. Verbs Followed by Two Objects: Fixed Order — 157
63. Verbs Followed by an Infinitive with Subject — 158
64. Verbs Followed by a Base Form with Subject — 160

Section 16 — 162-166
65. Verbs Followed by a Gerund with Subject — 162
66. Verbs Followed by NP (Object) + NP (Complement) — 163
67. Verbs Followed by NP (Object) + Adjective (Complement) — 164
68. The Use of *for* + an Infinitive with Subject — 165

Exercises for Sections 13-16 167-184

Summary Unit 185-188

Appendix 189-203
    I. English Noun Plurals 189
    II. Use of the Article *the* with Geographical Names 192
    III. Measures, Containers and Units for Foods and Household Commodities 195
    IV. Verbs and Adjectives Having Special Complements 197
    V. Participles Used as True Adjectives 202

Index 204

Answer Key 206

INTRODUCTORY UNIT

SENTENCES IN ENGLISH

Subject and predicate. Sentences in English have two parts: a subject and a predicate. The *subject* tells who (or what) performs the action of the verb. The *predicate* contains the verb and any other words that change or complete the meaning of the verb. These are examples of subjects and predicates.

SUBJECT	PREDICATE
Birds	sing.
The birds in the tree	are singing.
These apples	taste very good.
That girl's father	works in a hospital.

Sentence patterns. Sentences in English can be grouped into several types or kinds. We call these types *sentence patterns.* The subject is a constant factor in almost all sentences, so most of our sentence patterns are recognized by the different makeup of their predicates. Three sentence patterns which you have been using since early in your study of English are described below.

SENTENCE PATTERN NO. 1

SUBJECT—BE OR LINKING VERB—COMPLEMENT

BE and **linking verbs,** such as *become, seem, look,* connect or link their subject with a complement. The **complement** consists of the word or words which follow the verb. After *BE* and the *linking verbs,* the complement refers back to the subject of the sentence. The complement may be a noun, an adjective or an adverb.

If the complement is a noun, then the complement and the subject are the same person or thing.

    SUBJECT   COMPLEMENT
    His *father* is *president.* (noun)

If the complement is an adjective or adverb, the complement describes the subject or tells where it is.

    Her *father* became *famous.* (adjective)

    My *father* isn't *here.* (adverb)

SENTENCE PATTERN NO. 2
SUBJECT—TRANSITIVE VERB—DIRECT OBJECT

The **direct object** is an important kind of complement. It follows a verb and receives the action of a verb. A **transitive verb** is one that takes a direct object. These are examples of Sentence Pattern No. 2.

SUBJECT	TRANSITIVE VERB	DIRECT OBJECT
We	bought	some apples.
John	saw	a good movie.
Barbara	finished	her work.

SENTENCE PATTERN NO. 3
SUBJECT—INTRANSITIVE VERB

An **intransitive verb** is one which is not followed by an object. There may be adverbial modifiers after the verb, but these do not enter into the discussion of sentence patterns because they can also occur with transitive verbs.

SUBJECT	INTRANSITIVE VERB (& MODIFIERS)
Five old trees	fell.
We	listened (carefully).
The rain	started (all at once).

Noun phrase and verb phrase. In the sections above we referred to three sentence elements: *subject, direct object* and *noun complement*. These three elements can be studied at the same time because they are formed in the same way. All three are expressed by noun phrases. A **noun phrase** is a noun or something that can be substituted for a noun.

We can use the first letters of the two words **N**oun **P**hrase and refer to it as an **NP**.

A noun phrase, or NP, may be a noun (*men*), a pronoun (*you*), or it may consist of a group of words (*the men standing on the corner*).

Much of the grammar and practice in Sections 1 to 4 and 11 to 14 of this book will be concerned with the kinds of words and groups of words that form noun phrases.

A **verb phrase** consists of a verb and its tense and any other words that are associated with the verb. A verb phrase, or **VP,** functions as the predicate. We can say that a verb phrase consists of all the words that are not part of the noun phrase used as subject. A verb phrase may consist of one word or several words.

Special types of verb phrases are presented and practiced in Sections 9, 10, 15 and 16.

Sentence ⟶ Noun phrase (NP) + Verb phrase (VP). We may describe a sentence in English by saying it consists of a noun phrase followed by a verb phrase. We may write this as follows:

SENTENCE ⟶ NOUN PHRASE + VERB PHRASE

If we use the letter **S** (for Sentence), **NP** (for Noun phrase), and **VP** (for Verb phrase), we can define a sentence by means of this formula:

S ⟶ NP + VP

The verb phrase (VP) may contain another noun phrase (NP). This noun phrase may be used as the direct object of a transitive verb or as the complement after *BE* or a linking verb. We may describe certain verb phrases in this manner:

VERB PHRASE ⟶ VERB + NP

Here are examples of some English sentences:

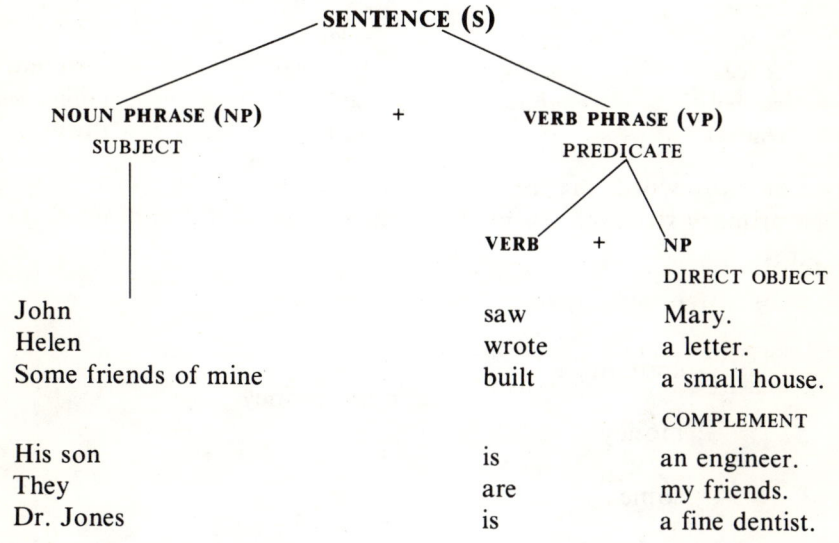

INTRODUCTORY UNIT 3

STRESS AND INTONATON

Stress is the loudness or force with which a syllable is spoken in English. We mark four levels of stress in this book—two strong stresses and two weak stresses. *Primary* and *secondary* are the names given to the two strong stresses. The two weak stresses are called *tertiary* and *weak*. The following marks are used to indicate the stresses:

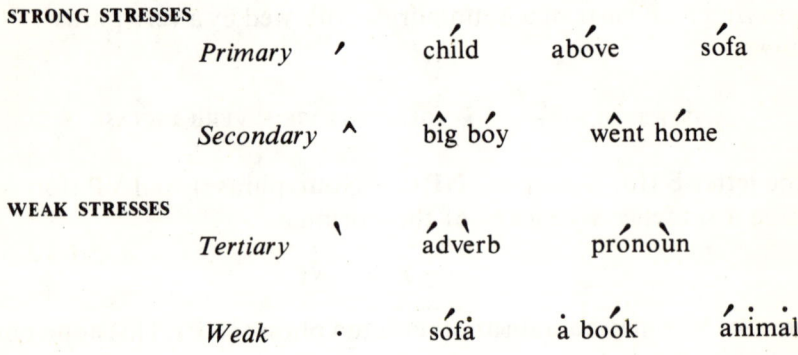

Every word in English has a stress pattern. These word stresses are shown in dictionaries. Here are a few word stress patterns for words pronounced *in isolation;* that is, by themselves, not grouped in phrases:

barber	alarm	exercise	animal
lesson	police	telephone	calendar
office	arrive	uniform	furniture
money	about	educate	languages
teacher	enough	satisfy	fluently

When two or more words are used together, only one of the words keeps its primary stress. The primary stress of the other word is reduced. In a phrase there is only one primary stress.

```
    IN ISOLATION         IN A PHRASE

      enóugh
              >          enôugh móney
      móney

      sóme
              >          sóme boóks
      boóks
```

This stress reduction generally takes place in a regular or predictable manner. Some of the drills and practices in this book deal with stress reduction.

Intonation is the rise and fall of the voice when speaking English. In this book the rise and fall is represented by three pitch levels (pitch 1, pitch 2 and pitch 3), joined by a solid line. Pitch levels do not represent the same absolute levels for all speakers. Everyone has his own range of pitch.

In a high percentage of statements and question-word questions, the voice begins on pitch level 2, rises to pitch level 3 on the syllable with primary stress and then steps down to pitch level 1 at the end of the sentence.

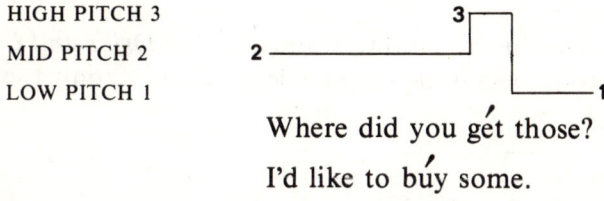

HIGH PITCH 3
MID PITCH 2
LOW PITCH 1

Where did you gét those?

I'd like to búy some.

If the stressed word of the phrase has only one syllable, the voice glides down. This glide is represented by a curved line.

Where did he gó?

When did they cóme?

In asking **Yes/No** questions, a rising question intonation is generally used. The voice usually begins on pitch level 2, goes to pitch 3 on the stressed syllable and then glides a little higher.

Are you leaving?   Did you tell them?

A sentence may consist of one phrase, or it may be composed of two or more phrases. In each phrase there is one word which is spoken with more force than the others. We use the primary stress mark (′) to indicate where this strong stress is located and refer to it as the *phrase* or *sentence stress*. When there is more than one phrase, the intonation usually rises to pitch 3 at each primary stress, but generally it goes down only to pitch level 2 at the end of each phrase until the last one is reached. On the final phrase the voice goes down to pitch level 1 and all sound of the voice stops. Note that we use a dotted vertical bar to separate the phrases.

(one phrase)   He came ín.

(two phrases)   He came in   and sat dówn.

(three phrases)   He came in   sat down   and began to tálk.
                  She went out got in the car and drove away.

INTRODUCTORY UNIT 5

Many sentences can be said either as one phrase or two phrases; that is, with one primary stress, or with two primary stresses.

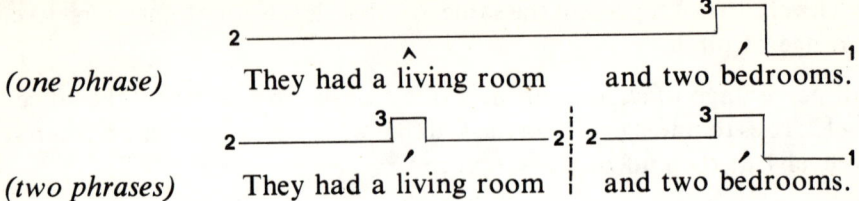

When intonation lines are used in this textbook and in *Extra Drills and Practices,* the intonation line is used without the numbered pitch levels. That is, only the solid line is used. These are examples.

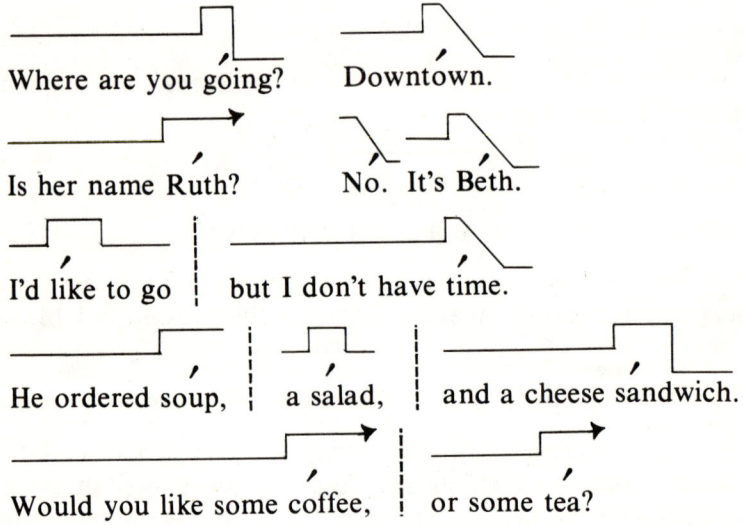

Often in these materials we mark only the phrase stress as an indication of the stress and intonation that is to be used.

    Are you leáving?

    Where are you góing?

    I'd líke to go, but I don't have tíme.

    He ordered júice, toást and cóffee.

It is important to know and remember that the stress marks and intonation lines can be used only as a rough guide as to the stresses and to the ups and downs of pitch. They give only a very general idea of how people actually speak. When you focus on stress and intonation in these materials, listen carefully to the teacher model sentences for you to reproduce, and use the marks and lines as clues as to what kind of stress and intonation is being used.

SECTION 1

Nouns
Count and Mass Nouns
Words Used as Both Count and Mass Nouns
Some Noun Modifiers
Noun Determiners
Articles and Demonstratives; "some," "any," "no"
Summary: Noun Phrases

1 Nouns

- **Nouns** form one of the large classes of words in English. Other large classes are adjectives, adverbs and verbs. Nouns name things or people (and also abstractions such as *honesty, strength,* etc.).

- Nouns can have different forms: singular, plural, singular possessive and plural possessive. Not all nouns have all of these possible forms.

    Most plurals are formed by adding the sounds /s/ , /z/ , or /iz/ to a singular noun.

    Extra Drill 1.1-2

    Some nouns form their plural in an irregular manner: *man-men, sheep-sheep, crisis-crises*. (For a more complete list of irregular nouns see the appendix, pages 189 to 191.

    Extra Drill 1.3

- **Proper nouns** are the names of specific people, places, organizations, events and objects.

    John Smith lives in *New York*.
    Mary saw the *Liberty Bell* last *July*.

    In writing, capital letters are generally used to begin each word of a proper noun. Words such as "of" and "the," however, are usually written with small letters.

    Helen   Buenos Aires
    Helen of Troy   the Isle of Capri
    the United Nations   New York City
    Tokyo

2 Count Nouns and Mass Nouns

> **Study these sentences.**
> 1. Milk, butter and cheese are dairy products.
> 2. Beans, peas and tomatoes are farm products.
> 3. I need a quart of milk and a loaf of bread.
> 4. We have a lot of room in our house.
> 5. We have a lot of rooms in our house.
> 6. Mrs. White baked two pies.
> 7. For dessert she served pie and ice cream.

- There are two important classes of nouns: count nouns and mass nouns. Nouns that have plurals are **count nouns.** These are things that are counted in English.

    seven pencils   six oranges
    two stores   five men

    > **Extra Drill 2.1-2**

- **Mass nouns** name things that are not counted in English. These are things that are measured in some way. They are not used with the words *a* and *an* or with numbers. Mass nouns are not used in the plural.

    Rice is grown in Asia.
    He has lots of *money.*
    Do you want some *sugar?*

    > **Extra Drill 2.3-4**

Mass nouns are also called *non-count nouns.*

These are examples of some of the mass nouns you have learned to use:

water	paper	food	chalk
milk	silk	clothing	soap
soup	wool	furniture	toothpaste
juice	cotton	laundry	money
ink	gold	medicine	music
oil	plastic	work	time

The names of many foods are mass nouns.

bread	sugar	fruit
meat	salt	grain
cheese	pepper	wheat
lettuce	coffee	rice
butter	tea	corn

> **Extra Drill 2.5-6**

> ### PRACTICE
>
> **Use *a little* with mass nouns; use *a few* with count nouns.**
>
> | TEACHER | STUDENT |
> |---|---|
> | 1. some chairs | *They need a few chairs.* |
> | 2. some help | *They need a little help.* |
> | 3. some money | .... |
> | 4. some pencils | .... |
> | 5. some time | .... |
> | 6. some rice | .... |
> | 7. some friends | .... |
> | 8. some stamps | .... |
> | 9. some information | .... |
> | 10. some textbooks | .... |

EXERCISE 2.1 | Count and Mass Nouns. See page 41.

- Types of containers or units of measure are often used with mass nouns to show amounts of a substance. These measures or containers are count nouns and can be either singular or plural. (For a more complete list of containers and units of measure see the appendix, page 195.)

    two *bottles* of ink   three *pieces* of paper
    a *loaf* of bread   two *pounds* of butter

EXERCISE 2.2 | Containers and Units of Measure with Mass Nouns. See page 41.   **Extra Drill 2.7-8**

3 Words Used as Both Mass and Count Nouns

- Some nouns are used as both count nouns and mass nouns. There is often a difference in meaning.

Paper used as a count noun means "a newspaper" or "a report".

    Mr. Jones takes two papers—a morning paper and an evening paper.
    They have asked me to read a paper at the meeting.

As a mass noun, *paper* refers to the substance or to "writing paper".

    Her new dress is made of paper.
    I forgot my notebook. Can you lend me some paper?

Light, room, business and *laundry* are examples of other nouns with different meanings when used as count and mass nouns.

EXERCISE 3.1 | Words Used as Both Count and Mass Nouns. See page 43.

> Extra Drill 3.1

- Words which refer to part of a whole, or to a class in general, are frequently mass nouns. The complete countable object, however, is usually a count noun.

    Some words of this type are *pie, cake, chicken, duck, turkey, ham, roast,* etc.

	USED AS COUNT NOUN	USED AS MASS NOUN
cake	Sally baked two cakes.	Would you like some cake?
chicken	She bought two frying chickens.	Please have some chicken.

    The noun *fish* is also used in this way. As a count noun the plural usually has no plural suffix; the form *fishes* is not often used.

    | *fish* | She also bought two fish. | Do you like to eat fish? |

- When a noun is used with the meaning of "a variety of" or "a kind of" almost any mass noun can be used as a count noun.

    This blend consists of three different *coffees*.
    Some *foods* are more important than others.

> Extra Drill 3.2

4 Some Noun Modifiers

- Nouns do not usually occur by themselves as subjects of sentences, as noun complements, or as objects of verbs. There are often other words used with the noun that describe or tell something about the noun. We call these words, or groups of words, **noun modifiers**.

    There are several different kinds of modifiers. Three of these are adjectives, nouns and noun possessives.

- **Adjectives** are words like *good, pretty, old, long, red,* etc. These words usually come directly before the noun they modify.

    | red shoes | old man |
    | pretty garden | long story |

> Extra Drill 4.1

- Many **nouns** can be used before other nouns as modifiers. They are called *premodifying nouns*.

    | *gold* ring | *brick* house |
    | *summer* pants | *state* police |

> Extra Drill 4.2-3

- **Noun possessives** can also be used as noun modifiers:

      John's hat   Mary's book   children's games

  A noun possessive comes before an adjective or premodifying noun:

      John's new hat   Mary's wool sweater

Extra Drill 4.4

EXERCISE 4.1 | Identifying Noun Modifiers. See page 43.

5 Noun Determiners

- There is a special and very important group of noun modifiers in English which we call **noun determiners.**

- These words introduce nouns. Many of them express amounts or quantities of the nouns that follow them. The noun determiners are words like *the, an, some, several, enough, another,* etc., all of which you have been using for some time.

- Not all noun determiners can be used before all nouns. The choice of a determiner depends on whether the following noun is singular or plural, and whether it is a count or mass noun.

The numeral *one,* for example, is used before singular count nouns. Other numerals (*two, three, four,* etc.) and the determiner *several* are used before plural count nouns. The possessive determiners (*my, your, his, her, its, our, their*) can be used before any kind of noun, singular, plural, or mass.

    one book   three tables
    another woman several men
    my sister   his friends   your health

Extra Drill 5.1

6 Articles and Demonstratives; *some, any, no*

- The definite article **the** is one of the few determiners that may be used before any noun. It is generally used before nouns that have been mentioned or identified in some way previously.

The is also used in situations where the referent is obvious.

    The sun is hot today, isn't it?
    (There's only one sun.)

    Andy bought a car last week, but the steering wheel was broken.
    (It must be the steering wheel of the car that Andy bought.)

The definite article is used with certain names, such as rivers (the Mississippi River), oceans (the Atlantic Ocean), seas (the Black Sea), deserts (the Gobi Desert), canals (the Panama Canal), buildings (the Empire State Building) and others.

The names of a few countries use *the,* for example, the Netherlands, the United Kingdom, the Philippines. (For a more complete list of names using *the* see the appendix, page 191.)

- The indefinite article *a,* or *an* (before vowel sounds), is used before singular count nouns that have not been mentioned or identified previously and there is no way to tell from the situation which one is meant. If there is only one chair in the room, you can tell someone: Please sit down in the chair. But if there are several chairs, you say: Please sit down in a chair.

EXERCISE 6.1 | Definite and Indefinite Articles. See page 44.

Extra Drill 6.1

- **Some** and **any** express indefinite quantities. They are used before either a mass noun or a plural count noun. *Some* is used in affirmative sentences and in some questions; *any* is used in negative sentences and in most questions.

    She went to the store to get *some sugar* and *some apples.*
    She bought *some lemons* but she didn't get *any oranges.*
    Do you need *some money?* Do you need *any help?*

Extra Drill 6.2-3

PRACTICE

Substitute progressively.

I need some money.

TEACHER	STUDENT
coffee	I need some coffee.
want	I want some coffee.
Negative Statement	I don't want any coffee.
she	She doesn't want any coffee.
tea	....
Past	....
buy	....
Affirmative Statement	....
oranges	....
bread	....
onions	....
Negative Statement	....
they	....
want	They didn't want any onions.

There is a slight difference in meaning between *some* and *any* when used in negative questions. When *some* is used *(Don't you need some help?)*, an affirmative answer is expected. With *any (Don't you need any help?)* a negative reply is expected.

This difference in meaning is similar to that expressed by the two kinds of tag questions.

EXPECTED ANSWER

Situation: Hearer obviously needs help.
Don't you need some help?
You need some help, don't you?   Yes.

Situation: Hearer probably doesn't need help.
Don't you need any help?
You don't need any help, do you?   No.

Extra Drill 6.4

- The word **no** is often used as a determiner in place of *not...any*.

    They do*n't* have *any* children.
    They have *no* children.

The word *no* is not used in a sentence or clause which has another negative.

PRACTICE

1. I don't have any money.
   I have no money.
2. She didn't buy any groceries.
   She bought no groceries.
3. We don't have any time.
   ....
4. He didn't grow any wheat.
   ....
5. She didn't have any food to eat.
   ....
6. We haven't had any rain this year.
   ....

Extra Drill 6.5

- *No + noun* (singular or plural) may also be used in subject position.

  No money was lost. *No speeches* were given. *No lady* would say that.

- The **demonstratives** are *this, that, these, those.* The words *this* and *that* are used before mass nouns and singular count nouns: *this man, this money, that book, that fruit.*

  These and *those* are used before plural count nouns: *these men, those books.*

- The interrogative words *which* and *what* are also used before nouns as determiners.

  Which movie did you see?   *What* book did you buy?

  We usually use *which* when asking to identify one of a known group.

  Which finger did you hurt?

  A: We were in Ecuador, Peru and Bolivia.
  B: *Which* country was the most interesting?

EXERCISE 6.2| Definite and Indefinite Determiners. See page 44.

7 Summary: Noun Phrases

- A **noun phrase (NP)** may consist of a count noun *(pencil, children),* a mass noun *(money, sugar),* or a proper noun *(Mary Smith, Alaska)* alone.

- A noun phrase may also consist of a noun with its modifiers. Noun modifiers include adjectives, other nouns, noun possessives and noun determiners.

  These are examples of noun phrases:

  | a man | red shoes | wool clothing | John's brother |
  | no money | tall men | steel furniture | Tokyo's population |

  A noun phrase may include more than one modifier.

  a tall man   some red shoes   his wool clothing   John's big brother

- In the sentence below, the italicized words *(words written this way)* are noun phrases.

  His family has *no money.*   *John* is *my brother.*
  Mary's wearing *red shoes.*   *Bill* has *two sisters.*
  That stone bridge is very old.   *Canada* is *a beautiful country.*
  John's sister has *several children.* Do *his parents* have *money?*
  Those two boys are *brothers.*   *His sister's name* is *June.*

EXERCISE 7.1| Identifying Noun Phrases. See page 45.

SECTION 2

Noun Modifiers: Prepositional Phrases
Pronouns
Noun Determiners: "more" and "most;" "enough;" "plenty of"
Noun Determiners: "(a) little/(a) few;" "a lot of" and "lots of;"
"much/many;" "a great (good) deal of"
Noun Substitutes
Summary: Noun Phrases

8 Noun Modifiers—Prepositional Phrases

- A **prepositional phrase** consists of a preposition (*in, to, with,* etc.) and a noun phrase. These are examples of prepositional phrases:

    in the summer   with red hair
    on the corner   over his head

    A noun phrase that is used after a preposition is called the **object** of the preposition.

- A prepositional phrase may function as a noun modifier. When it does so, it follows the noun.

    The man *on the corner* is my uncle. (modifies *man*)
    The lesson *on page six* is quite easy. (modifies *lesson*)

Extra Drill 8.1-2

PRACTICE

Substitute progressively.

The man on the corner waved to us.

TEACHER	STUDENT
in the black coat	The man in the black coat waved to us.
the woman	....
in the blue suit	....
see us	....
in the green hat	....
the lady	....
Yes/No Question	Did the lady in the green hat see us?
with the red hair	....
call us	....
with the long nose	....
in the white dress	....
notice us	....
Negative Statement	The lady in the white dress didn't notice us.

- A noun phrase (NP) may consist of a noun with all its modifiers. Therefore NP + prepositional phrase = noun phrase.

  The italicized words in the sentence below are NPs.
  The girl with red hair is Janet.
  The lesson on page six is quite easy.
  Picnics by the river are fun.

Extra Drill 8.3

EXERCISE 8.1 | Prepositional Phrases Used as NP Modifiers. See page 45.

9 Pronouns

- A noun phrase may consist of a **personal pronoun.**

- **Subject pronouns** *(I, you, he, she, it, we, they)* are used, as the name suggests, as subjects of verbs.

- When replacing singular nouns, *he* is used for a male person, *she* for a female person, and *it* for a thing. The form for plural persons and things is *they*. When referring to animals, the pronouns *it* (or *they*) are generally used, although it is not unusual to hear the pronouns *he* and *she* if the animals have names.

- **Object pronouns** are used as the objects of verbs or prepositions. The object pronouns are *me, you, him, her, it, us, them.*

  An object pronoun may be used as the indirect object of a verb as well as the *direct object.* In the sentence *John gave her the book,* the pronoun "her" is used as the indirect object.

- A pronoun may be used to replace a noun and its modifiers; that is, a noun phrase:

  <u>The two men</u> saw <u>the woman in the red hat.</u>
     They   saw   her.

PRACTICE

Replace the italicized words with pronouns.

MARY	My mother and father are going to take a trip.
JOHN	When are *your parents* going to take *the trip*?
MARY	Next month. Billy wants to go, too.
JOHN	Your parents aren't going to take *your baby brother,* are they?
MARY	Oh, no. *Billy* can't go.
JOHN	Will you do the cooking while *your parents* are gone?
MARY	No, but I'll help. My older sister Ruth will do most of the cooking. *She and I* will be able to keep things going.
JOHN	Is *Ruth* a good cook?
MARY	Oh, my, yes. Janie says she's going to help, too.
JOHN	*Your little sister* can't cook, can she?
MARY	No, *Janie* and her friend tried to make some candy last week, but it was awful.
JOHN	What did you do with *the candy?*
MARY	*The children* poured it out before Mother got home. *Mother* didn't think it was funny at all.

EXERCISE 9.1 | Practice with Pronouns. See page 46.

Extra Drill 9.1-2

10 Noun Determiners: *more* and *most; enough; plenty of*

- The determiners **more** and **most** compare quantities. Both are used before mass nouns and plural count nouns. *More* means "a larger quantity"; *most* means "a majority" or "more than half".

> *More people* live in the city than in the country.
> Do you need *more money?*
> *Most children* like fruit.
> I like *most movies.*

Most is often preceded by *the*. *The most* expresses the greatest quantity.

> I think bankers make *the most money.*
> Which class has *the most children?*

More and *most* are often followed by *of* + *determiner* when definite nouns are being referred to.

> *More of the* students here come from Chicago than from any other city.
> *Most of my* friends are also university students.

- **Enough,** meaning "sufficient", can be used either before or after the noun it modifies. *I have enough time* and *I have time enough* mean the same thing. The noun determiner *enough* is used before mass nouns and plural count nouns.

Extra Drill 10.1-2

PRACTICE

Practice this dialog.

NANCY	Do you want some things from the store, Mother?
MOTHER	Yes. Get a few bananas and some more sugar, will you?
NANCY	Do you have enough coffee?
MOTHER	Yes. I think we have coffee enough. But perhaps you'd better get a few onions. Most of these onions are spoiled.
NANCY	Shall I get more potatoes?
MOTHER	Yes. Do you have money enough?
NANCY	No, I'm sure I don't.
MOTHER	All right, here is some more. Hurry back so I can get dinner started.

- The determiner **plenty of** is used before both mass and plural count nouns. It means "more than enough," "as much as one could want." It is almost always used in affirmative sentences.

> We have *plenty of* coffee but not enough doughnuts.

11 Noun Determiners: *a lot of* and *lots of; much/many; (a) little/(a) few; a great (good) deal of*

> **Study these sentences.**
> 1. He has a lot of friends.
> 2. They have lots of money.
> 3. A lot of people came to the meeting.
> 4. He doesn't have much money.
> 5. They don't have many friends.
> 6. Do you read many books?
> 7. Not many people came to the lecture.
> 8. He has a lot of money but few friends.
> 9. I'll have a little time this afternoon.
> 10. I don't have a great deal of interest in music.

- **A lot of** and **lots of** mean the same thing. They are indefinite determiners which express a large amount. Both are used before mass nouns and plural count nouns.

    a lot of sugar   lots of children
    lots of sugar   a lot of children

Both expressions are used a great deal more in informal speech than they are in formal writing. They commonly replace *much* in affirmative statements.

    He needs a lot of money. (instead of "He needs much money.")

> **Extra Drill 11.1**

- **Much** and **many** are indefinite determiners. *Much* is used before mass nouns (*much money*); *many* is used before count nouns (*many friends*).

In informal speech *much* and *many* are generally used in negative statements and in questions. They are often replaced by *a lot of* or *lots of* in affirmative statements.

    Does he need much money?   He doesn't have many friends.
    But he has lots of relatives. (*or* "He has many relatives.")

Negation may also be expressed by using *not* before *much* and *many* in subject position.

    Not much time was lost.   *Not many people* came.

- The adverb *very* is frequently used before *much* and *many*.

> **Extra Drill 11.2**

    I don't have *very much time*.   *Not very many people* came.

SECTION TWO

- **Little** and **a little** are used before mass nouns to show a small amount. **Few** and **a few** are used before plural count nouns.

- *Little* and *few* express a negative idea; they emphasize how small the amount is. *A little* and *a few* are more positive in meaning.

   If we say *John has little interest in music,* we mean that he has practically no interest in it. If we say *He has a little interest in music,* we mean that he has some interest in it.

   Extra Drill 11.3

- The expression **little or no** also has a negative meaning.

   He has little or no interest in music.

- **A great deal of** and **a good deal of** are used to express a large quantity. Both expressions are used only before mass nouns. **A good deal of** is not used with negative verbs. On the other end of the scale, **a little bit of** expresses a small quantity of a mass noun.

   I've heard he has a great deal of money.
   He's spent a good deal of time in New York.
   We had only a little bit of time left.

   EXERCISE 11.1 | Noun Determiners Indicating Great and Little Quantity. See page 46.
   EXERCISE 11.2 | Summary Exercise: Noun Determiners. See page 47.

12 Noun Substitutes

- Most of the determiners (except articles) can be used without a following noun. When they are used in this way, they are called **noun substitutes,** and they replace an entire noun phrase.

   Much and *a little* are used to replace mass nouns. *Many* and *a few* are used to replace plural count nouns.

   Extra Drill 12.1

	NOUN SUBSTITUTE
Does he have *any friends?*	Yes, he has *a few.*
Do you need *any money?*	Yes, I could use *a little.*
Would you like *some meat?*	Yes, but don't give me *much.*
Have you seen *any good movies* lately?	No, not *many.*

   Some and *any* are used as noun substitutes, as are *several, enough, more,* and *the most,* and numerals.

   He offered me *some candy,* but I didn't want *any.*
   There were *a lot of children* there. *Several* were playing basketball.
   Would you like *more coffee?* No, I've had *enough,* thank you.
   I don't like *vegetables,* but I ate *some.*

- The determiner *no (no money, no pencils)* does not occur as a noun substitute. Instead the word *none* is used.

  He has *no money*.   He has *none* at all.

> **PRACTICE**
>
> **Answer the questions.**
>
> | SPEAKER A | SPEAKER B |
> |---|---|
> | 1. Do you have any money? | No, I have no money. I have none at all. |
> | 2. Do you have any time? | No, ... |
> | 3. Do they have any friends? | No, ... |
> | 4. Is there any butter? | No, ... |
> | 5. Does he have any savings? | No, ... |
> | 6. Did he have any supper? | No, ... |

- The determiners with *of, (lots of, a lot of, a great deal of, plenty of,* etc.) are used without the word *of* when they occur as noun substitutes.

  Does he have much money?   Yes, he has *lots*.
                                        he has *a lot*.
                                        he has *a great deal*.
                                        he has *a good deal*.

- The demonstratives *this, that, these* and *those* can be used without a following noun as noun substitutes.

  When *this* and *that* refer to something specific, they are commonly used with the word *one*. If they refer to something general, such as an idea or situation, or to a mass noun, *one* is not used.

Which horse did he choose?	*That* one.
This pen is no good.	Try *this* one.
I never wanted to come.	*That* wasn't my idea.
Did he forget the paint too?	No, he didn't forget *that*.

  These and *those* are never followed by *one* or *ones*.

  These apples are good but *those* are better.

  Extra Drill 12.2

- The possessive form of a noun, singular or plural, may also be used without a following noun.

>   That's my coat. It isn't *John's*.
>   Whose car is that? It's the *Johnsons'*.

- Pronouns have a special form when they replace possessives and the following noun: *mine, yours, his, hers, its, ours, theirs*. The word *whose* is also used without a following noun.

| Extra Drill 12.3 |

>   That wasn't your idea, It was *mine*.
>   That book isn't *hers*, or *his*, or *mine*. I don't know *whose* it is.

EXERCISE 12.1| Practice with Possessive Pronouns. See page 47.

EXERCISE 12.2| Noun Substitutes. See page 47.

13 Summary: Noun Phrases

- An *NP + a prepositional phrase* is one kind of noun phrase. These are examples:

>   those pretty women with their new dresses   the boy at his desk
>   that tall building on the next corner   the book on the table

- A noun phrase may consist of a subject or object pronoun.

>   *He* called *us*. *We* saw *them*.   *I* gave *it* to *him*.

- A noun phrase may consist of a noun substitute. The italicized words are noun phrases.

>   A lot of people came. *Several* were professors.
>   Nineteen children passed the exam. *Four* failed.
>   Several people were invited. *Not very many* came.
>   I like coffee, but I don't drink *a great deal*.

- Possessive forms of nouns and pronouns are both used as noun phrases.

>   My car's in the garage. Let's take *yours*.
>   Is that your bicycle? No, it's *Jack's*.

- The italicized words in the sentences below are noun phrases.

>   I wanted *some coffee*, but *the grocer* didn't have *any*.
>   *The red flowers in your garden* are beautiful.
>   Do *you* like *tea with sugar*?
>   *Dr. Jones* gave *a lecture on food*.
>   Would *you* like *some carrots*? Yes, *a few*, please.

EXERCISE 13.1| Identifying Noun Phrases. See page 48.

EXERCISE 13.2| Summary Exercise Practice with Noun Determiners and Noun Substitutes. See page 48.

SECTION 3

Adjective Precedence
Noun Determiners: "some" and "any" with Strong Stress
Noun Determiners: "either/neither;" "another/other;" "each" and "every"
Indefinite Pronouns
Summary: Noun Phrases

14 Adjective Precedence

- One very common combination of modifiers is a noun determiner followed by an adjective.

    a big boy   *other long* tables   *several older* boys

- Two or more adjectives may modify a noun. Often it does not make any difference which adjective comes first or second. With some kinds of adjectives, however, there is a definite order which is followed.

Here are three kinds of adjectives and the order in which they are generally used before a noun: (1) descriptive adjectives (*beautiful, delicious, interesting,* etc.); (2) size or age adjectives *(little, old, young, new);* (3) colors such as *red, green, white,* etc. When two or three of these kinds of adjectives are used to modify a noun, then their order is as follows:

NOUN DETERMINER	(1) DESCRIPTIVE ADJECTIVE	(2) SIZE OR AGE ADJECTIVE	(3) COLOR	NOUN
an	interesting	old	red	book
the	beautiful	little	white	house
some	comfortable	new	green	chairs

> **PRACTICE**
>
> 1. The white house was beautiful.
>   It was a beautiful white house.
> 2. The new chairs were comfortable.
>   They were comfortable new chairs.
> 3. The red apples were delicious.
>   They were ....
> 4. The new book was interesting.
>   It was ....
> 5. The little boy was intelligent.
>   He was ....
> 6. The green pears were big.
>   They were ....
> 7. The little bottle was pretty.
>   It was ....

EXERCISE 14.1 | Word Order. See page 49.

Extra Drill 14.1-2

- An adjective of *nationality* (*French, Spanish,* etc.) or other word denoting *origin* or style (*southern, downtown, New York,* etc.) is generally the last kind of adjective in order before the noun being modified.

> She bought a beautiful old *French* painting.
> He's a famous young *Brazilian* writer.
> We found some fine new red *Thai* silk.
> Miller wrote about his *New England* boyhood.

EXERCISE 14.2 | Adjective Precedence with Origin Modifiers. See page 49.

Extra Drill 14.3

15 Noun Determiners: *some* and *any* with Strong Stress

- **Some** and **any,** spoken with weak stress, are used before mass nouns and plural count nouns to express an indefinite amount.

> sóme boóks   sóme cóffee
> some men   some sugar
> some chairs   some money

- When *some* is spoken with strong stress, it may be used before singular nouns (as well as plural and mass nouns).

> sôme mán   Sôme mán is at the door.
> sôme lády   Sôme lády called on the telephone.

24   GRAMMAR AND DRILLBOOK

In each of the sentences above, "some" refers to a specific person, but the person is unidentified. That is, the speaker doesn't know who it is.

>
> ## PRACTICE
>
> | | TEACHER | STUDENT |
> |---|---|---|
> | 1. | Who called?
 a man | Sŏme mán.
 I'm not sure whó it was. |
> | 2. | Who's at the door?
 a lady | Sŏme lády.
 I'm not sure whó it is. |
> | 3. | Who answered the telephone?
 a little child | ....
 .... |
> | 4. | Who was driving the car?
 a woman | ....
 .... |
> | 5. | Who won the money?
 a little old lady | ....
 .... |
> | 6. | Who's calling?
 a girl | ....
 .... |

- **Any,** spoken with strong stress, may also be used before singular nouns. It has two or three different meanings, depending on context. It may mean "every" *(Ăny mŏther will protect her child)*; or it may mean "one out of many" or "no matter which" *(You may have ăny péncil; You may write a composition on ăny súbject).*

> **Extra Drill 15.1**

- Before plural nouns, *some* with strong stress contrasts one group of people or things with another. It is commonly used in conjunction with the determiner *other*.

    Sŏme péople came early; ŏther péople came late.
    Sŏme mên were brave; ŏther mên were weak.

16 Noun Determiners: *either/neither; another/other; each* and *every*

- The determiners **either** and **neither** make a choice between two things. *Neither* is negative; it is not used with negative verb forms.

    You may have either book.
    Neither child would talk to me.

> **Extra Drill 16.1**

- As noun substitutes, *either* and *neither* may be used by themselves, or they may be followed by *one:* **either one, neither one.**

  Which do you want? I don't want *either*.
   (or) I don't want *either one*.

  Did Jack or Bill telephone? No, *neither* called.
   (or) No, *neither one* called.

PRACTICE

SPEAKER A SPEAKER B

(respond negatively as in the model)

1. Which of these two balls does he want? (either) He doesn't want either one. He has a ball.

2. Which of these two pencils do you want? (neither) Neither one. I have a pencil.

3. Which of these two pens does she want? (either) ....

4. Which of these two dictionaries does he want? (neither) ....

5. Which of these two alarm clocks do you want? (neither) ....

6. Which of these two umbrellas does she want? (either) ....

Either and **either one** may also be used in affirmative answers.

Who knows about the advertising rates—Nelson or Riviera?
You can ask *either one*.

- **Another** and **other** are *indefinite noun determiners. Another,* which means "a different one" or "an additional one," is used before singular nouns.

  I needed *another* week to finish. They moved to *another* house.

26 GRAMMAR AND DRILLBOOK

PRACTICE

	SPEAKER A	SPEAKER B
1.	Would you like some more coffee? (cup)	Yes, please. I think I'll have another cup.
2.	Would you like some more fruit? (apple)	Yes, please. I think I'll have another apple.
3.	Would you like some more milk? (glass)	....
4.	Would you like some more bread? (slice)	....
5.	Would you like some more meat? (lamb chop)	....
6.	Would you like some more ice cream? (dish)	....
7.	Would you like some more chicken? (piece)	....

EXERCISE 16.1 | Definite and Indefinite Noun Substitutes. See page 50.

- *Other,* meaning "the remaining ones," or "different ones," is used before plural count nouns and mass nouns.

    Some people were talking; *other* people were listening.

- *Other* is used with definite noun determiners to form combinations such as *the other, my other, every other, this other, that other* before singular nouns.

    the other house   that other man   every other person

Definite determiners that are used with plural count nouns and mass nouns may also precede *other.*

    those other men   the other information   his other sisters

- Because *other* follows the definite determiners, it is often called a **postdeterminer.**

SUMMARY: *another, other, the other*

	SINGULAR COUNT NOUN	PLURAL COUNT NOUN	MASS NOUN
INDEFINITE	**another** book	**other** books	**other** information
DEFINITE	**the other** book	**the other** books	**the other** information

SECTION THREE

- As indefinite noun substitutes, **another** or **another one** is used to replace singular nouns. **Others** or **other ones** replaces plural nouns, and these may be preceded by noun determiners such as *some* or *a few*.

    Do you like apples? Yes, please give me *another*.
    (or) Yes, please give me *another one*.

    Do you like these neckties? Yes, but please show me a few *others*.
    (or) Yes, but please show me some *other ones*.

INDEFINITE COUNT NOUN SUBSTITUTES

SINGULAR COUNT NOUN	PLURAL COUNT NOUN
Give me **another**.	Some days seem long; **others** seem short.
I took **another one**.	Ted buys jazz records; I prefer **other ones**.

Extra Drill 16.2

- As *definite noun substitutes,* **the other** or **the other one** is used to replace singular nouns.

    One boy stayed. *The other* left.
    (or) *The other one* left.

To replace plural count nouns, either **the others** or **the other ones** may be used.

   These shoes don't fit very well. I'll take *the others*.
   I don't think these apples are as good as *the other ones*.

DEFINITE COUNT NOUN SUBSTITUTES

SINGULAR COUNT NOUN	PLURAL COUNT NOUN
One boy stayed; **the other** left.	Ask **the others** to come.
Give me **the other one**.	These apples are no good. Let's buy **the other ones**.

Extra Drill 16.3

PRACTICE

	SPEAKER A	SPEAKER B
1.	Don't you like this bicycle?	Yes, but I believe I like the other one better. (or *the other*)
2.	Doesn't she like these chairs?	Yes, but I believe she likes the other ones better. (or *the others*)
3.	Don't you like this restaurant?	....
4.	Doesn't he like these paintings?	....
5.	Doesn't she like these paintings?	....
6.	Don't you like this hotel?	....
7.	Doesn't she like this bakery?	....
8.	Don't you like these ice skates?	....

EXERCISE 16.2 | Definite and Indefinite Noun Substitutes. See page 50.

- As substitutes for mass nouns we use **some other** (indefinite) and **the other** (definite).

MASS NOUN SUBSTITUTES

INDEFINITE	I don't like this paper; show me *some other*.
DEFINITE	I don't like that coffee; I prefer *the other*.

- Another common definite noun substitute is **the rest.** We use it for both count and mass nouns. With count nouns it must refer to three or more; it cannot refer to only one or two.

    If you'll do half of the work, I'll do *the rest*.
    Tommy found six Easter eggs, and Betty found *the other two*. (not *the rest*)
    Betty found two of the Easter eggs, and Tommy found *the rest*.
    Some eggs were blue, some others were red and *the rest* were yellow.

- **Each** and **every** are definite determiners used before singular nouns.

    The teacher gave a book to *every child* in the class.
    Now *each child* has his own book.

    Extra Drill 16.4

- **Each** or **each one** may be used as a noun substitute.

    She offered some candy to the children.   *Each* took a piece.
    (or) *Each one* took a piece.

- **Every one** (with stress on *óne*) means "all the members of a group considered individually." The group must consist of three or more.

      There were twelve apples.   The boys ate *every óne*.

      I opened two cans of vegetables.   *Each óne* was spoiled.
                                                                         (or) *Both* were spoiled.*

      Jim tried all the grapes.   *Every óne* was sour.

*See Point 19.

Extra Drill 16.5

- In summary, we note that certain determiners may be followed by the word *one* when used as noun substitutes.

They are: *another, the other, each, either* and *neither*. The interrogative word *which* may also be followed by *one: Which do you want?* or *Which one do you want?*

As a noun substitute, the word *every* must be followed by *one*. This is also true of the demonstratives *this* and *that* when they refer to something specific.

EXERCISE 16.3 | Determiners and Noun Substitutes. See page 51.

17 Indefinite Pronouns

> **Study these sentences.**
> 1. Do you know everyone?
> 2. There's somebody at the door.
> 3. Nobody told me about it.
> 4. Here's somebody's hat.
> 5. I won't tell anyone else.
> 6. This is somebody else's hat; it isn't mine.
> 7. Do you know anyone famous?
> 8. Someone at the door wants to speak with you.

- **Indefinite pronouns** are used as noun phrases.

  INDEFINITE PRONOUNS

anyone	anybody	anything
everyone	everybody	everything
someone	somebody	something
no one	nobody	nothing

  Extra Drill 17.1

  As with other noun phrases, they may function as the subject or object of a verb or as the object of a preposition. -*one* and -*body* have the same meaning: "person;" -*thing* refers to inanimates and non-humans.

- These pronouns are singular. They have no plural form, but those formed with -*one* and -*body* may be made possessive.

  somebody's book   everyone's hope   nobody's business

- The words with *some-* are used in affirmative sentences and in some questions. Words with *any-* are used in negative sentences and in most questions. Words with *every-* may be used in both affirmative and negative sentences and in all questions.

  Did you meet anyone (someone) there?
  Yes, I met everyone, but I didn't eat anything.
  Did you meet everyone?
  I met a few, but I didn't meet everybody.

  Extra Drill 17.2-3

  The words with *any-* can be used in affirmative sentences when their meaning is "no matter who," or "no matter which."

  It doesn't matter who you are. With practice, *anybody* can learn to speak English.
  You can have *anything* you want.

- All these pronouns can be followed by the word *else* which means "different" or "additional." The word *else* can be made possessive when a possessive is desired.

  The pens were cheap. *Everything else* was expensive.
  I saw Mr. Smith, but I didn't see *anyone else*.
  That isn't my pen. It belongs to *someone else*. It's *somebody else's*.

  Extra Drill 17.4

- Indefinite pronouns may be modified by adjectives, prepositional phrases and clauses. These types of modifiers follow the indefinite pronoun.

anything *sweet*	everyone *in the world*	everything *that I saw*
something *strange*	somebody *at the party*	anybody *that knows*
no one *interesting*	nothing *of interest*	someone *who cares a lot*

EXERCISE 17.1 | Indefinite Pronouns. See page 51.
EXERCISE 17.2 | Indefinite Pronouns + *else*. See page 52.

Extra Drill 17.5-6

18 Summary: Noun Phrases

- A noun phrase may consist of a noun and its modifiers. There may be several noun modifiers. The italicized words are examples of noun phrases (NP's).

    They bought *a beautiful little white house.*
    The big brown building on the corner is the bank.
    Do you know *that other man with the white hair?*

- Noun substitutes are used as NPs.

    I think I'll buy *the other one.*
    Several children came to the party. *Each* brought a gift.
    Neither liked the food.

- Indefinite pronouns, with and without modifiers, are used as NPs.

    Do you want *something?*
    I didn't buy *anything else.*
    Everyone in the world knows that. *Anyone* knows that.

EXERCISE 18.1 | Identifying Noun Phrases. See page 52.

SECTION 4

Noun Determiners: "all (the)" and "both (the)"
Predeterminers
Adjective + "one" or "ones"
Pre-noun Modifiers: Summary Chart
Summary: Noun Phrases

19 Noun Determiners: *both (the)* and *all (the)*

- **Both** (or **both the**) is used when referring to exactly two people or things. *Both* is not used before mass nouns.

 Both children asked a lot of questions.
 Both the girls were quite pretty.

When *both* modifies the subject of a sentence, it may be used (1) before the noun, (2) before the main verb, or (3) after forms of *be: am, is, are, was, were*.

There is no difference in meaning between these pairs of sentences:

Both boys eat a lot.	Both the children were good.
The boys both eat a lot.	The children were both good.

PRACTICE

1. Both boys came early.
 The boys both came early.
2. Both pens are good.
 The pens are both good.
3. Both experiments failed.
 ....
4. Both answers were wrong.
 ....
5. Both invitations arrived late.
 ....
6. Both libraries have several thousand books.
 ....
7. Both mirrors were broken.
 ....
8. Both mechanics do good work.
 ....

- There must be at least three things or people being discussed in order to use **all** or **all the**. *All* is used with mass nouns and count nouns.

    When *all the* is used, it means the whole group of things or people that are being talked about: *All the men were strong; All the food was spoiled.*

    All (without *the*) carries a "universal" meaning; that is, the statement is true in every situation. The negative of this is expressed with *not all*.

    > *All* fish can swim, but *not all* birds can fly.

    EXERCISE 19.1 | *All* and *all the* + NP. See page 53.

- When *all* or *both* modify the subject of a sentence, they may be used before the noun, or they may occur after an auxiliary and before the main verb. These two sentences both mean the same thing:

    | Extra Drill 19.1 |

    > All birds can sing.   Both twins will go.
    > Birds can all sing.   The twins will both go.

    All and *both* follow the object pronouns.

    > I saw *them all*.   He told *us both*.

    If a pronoun is used as subject, the usual position for *all* and *both* is before the main verb, or after an auxiliary or verb *BE*.

    > They will both go.   They can all come.   They were both here.

    | Extra Drill 19.2 |

    In short answers, *all* and *both* go between the pronoun and auxiliary.

    > Yes, they all did.   Yes, we both were.

- The determiner **each,** as we have seen, precedes a singular noun: *Each boy has a knife. He gave some money to each child.*

    With a plural subject, *each* precedes the main verb or follows the first auxiliary.

    > Each teacher gave a talk.
    > The teachers each gave a talk.

    > Each house was being painted white.
    > The houses were each being painted white.

> ## PRACTICE
>
> 1. Each man gave a report.
>   *The men each gave a report.*
> 2. Each photographer took several pictures.
>   *The photographers each took several pictures.*
> 3. Each experiment took several years.
>   ....
> 4. Each child wrote a composition.
>   ....
> 5. Each nurse works eight hours.
>   ....
> 6. Each example was written on the blackboard.
>   ....

EXERCISE 19.2 | Summary Exercise: Practice with Noun Determiners. See page 53.

20 Predeterminers

- Most noun determiners can be followed by the word *of* (*some of, a few of, much of,* etc.) Appropriate expressions of this kind can be used before a definite determiner (*the, his, those,* etc.) followed by a mass noun or plural count noun. They are called **predeterminers**.

BEFORE MASS NOUNS	BEFORE PLURAL COUNT NOUNS
much of the water	many of the boys
a lot of his money	several of these books
a little of the medicine	a few of the women
all of the music	both of the children
	either (one) of the pens
	neither (one) of his sisters
	each (one) of the boys
	every one of the boys

Each, either and *neither* may be used alone or with *one. Every* must be followed by *one* when used with *of.* As subjects they take singular verb forms.

    Each (one) of the boys has his own bicycle.
    Every one of his toys is broken.

    All of the children were crying.
    Every one of the children was crying.

> Extra Drill 20.1-2

- After a mass noun predeterminer, *it* can replace the determiner + mass noun:

    much of *the water*   much of *it*
    a lot of *his money*   a lot of *it*
    all of *the music*   all of *it*

After a count noun predeterminer, *them* replaces the determiner + plural count noun:

    many of *the boys*   many of *them*
    neither of *his sisters*   neither of *them*
    every one of *the children*   every one of *them*

| Extra Drill 20.3 |

This, that, these, those and the possessive pronoun forms *mine, yours,* etc. can be used after predeterminers.

    Have some of *my ice cream.*   Try some of *mine.*
    Get some of *those apples.*   Buy some of *those.*

- The word *both* may be followed by a possessive word or by *these* and *those.*

    both my sisters   both those movies

PRACTICE

Repeat, with substitutions.

1. I'd like to read ....
    - those three books on science
    - your other books on music
    - all your books on art
    - both those books on farming
    - all those other books on engineering

2. Have you met ....?
    - my two sisters
    - my other brother
    - all my brothers and sisters
    - both my parents
    - my other two friends

EXERCISE 20.1 | Summary Exercise: Practice with Determiners and Predeterminers. See page 54.
EXERCISE 20.2 | Practice with Predeterminers. See page 55.
EXERCISE 20.3 | Substitute Forms After Predeterminers. See page 55.

21 Adjectives + *one* or *ones*

- The words **one** and **ones** can be used to replace count nouns that occur after adjectives. *One* is used in place of singular nouns; *ones* replaces plural nouns. Study these sentences:

    John lives in a *white house*. Bill lives in a *red one*.
    I don't like *short pencils*. I prefer *long ones*.

    > Extra Drill 21.1

    > PRACTICE
    >
    > 1. Mr. White has a green car.
    >   (white) Mr. Green has *a white one*.
    > 2. I never read long books.
    >   (short) I always read *short ones*.
    > 3. The big children went to the movies.
    >   (little) The .... had to stay home.
    > 4. I never take the late train.
    >   (early) I always ....
    > 5. Jim doesn't like to wear his new shoes.
    >   (old) He always wears ....
    > 6. They don't like living in a big house.
    >   (small) They prefer ....

- Determiners like *the, these* and *those, any, which, what* and *whose* may all occur before numerals. Possessive determiners may also be used in this position.

    | the two men | those six people |
    | those nine boys | any seven women |
    | which two boys? | my two sons |

- *Other* may come before or after a number:

    | the two other rooms | those other five boys |
    | the other two rooms | the six other children |

- The determiner *all* may be followed by a numeral, a possessive word, or by *other, the other, this, that, these* and *those*.

    | all my life | all those men |
    | all six children | all other people |
    | all this coffee | all that time |

SECTION FOUR

22 Pre-Noun Modifiers (Summary)

- When there are two or more modifiers for a single noun, these modifiers usually come in a certain order shown by the following chart. Of course, it is seldom that a noun would have all types of modifiers at once, but two examples are given in the chart.

PRE-NOUN MODIFIERS									
DETERMINERS			ADJECTIVES					
PRE-DETERMINER	DETERMINER	POST-DETERMINER, CARDINAL NO.	DESCRIPTIVE	SIZE OR AGE	COLOR	ORIGIN	PRE-MODIFYING NOUN	MODIFIED NOUN
All of	our	other ten	warm	little	brown	Russian	fur	hats
None of	the	last three	valuable	old	white	oriental	marble	blocks

EXERCISE 22.1 | Position of Origin Modifiers. See page 56.

Extra Drill 22.1

23 Summary: Noun Phrases

- In the preceding sections we have studied some of the kinds of words and groups of words that are used as noun phrases.

  Nouns, indefinite pronouns, and noun substitutes are used as noun phrases, alone and with modifiers. Subject and object pronouns, possessive nouns and possessive pronouns are also used as NPs.

- Noun phrases may function as subjects, as complements after *BE* and linking verbs, as direct objects after transitive verbs, and as objects of prepositions.

- Below are examples of noun phrases used as **subjects.** Notice the type of word used as the main word of the subject NP in each case.

```
                              SENTENCE (S)
                             /            \
                 NOUN PHRASE (NP)    +    VERB PHRASE (VP)
                    SUBJECT                  PREDICATE
```

NAME	*John*	came early.
MASS NOUN	The *money*	was lost.
MASS NOUN	The *money* on the table	is your change.
COUNT NOUN	The two little *boys* in short pants	are my brothers.
INDEF. PRONOUN	*Everyone* in the world	knows that.
NOUN SUBSTITUTE	*Some* of the engineers	left early.
POSS. PRONOUN	*Mine*	is the blue one.
PRONOUN	*He*	can't come.
POSS. NOUN	*Miss Green's*	are the same as mine.
NOUN SUBSTITUTE	A great *deal*	was said about taxes.

- Below are examples of noun phrases used as **complements** after the verb. Identify the type of word used as the main word of the complement NP.

```
                              SENTENCE (S)
                             /            \
                 NOUN PHRASE (NP)    +    VERB PHRASE (VP)
                    SUBJECT                  PREDICATE
                                     /              \
                                 VERB BE    +    NOUN PHRASE (NP)
                                                  COMPLEMENT
```

			TYPE OF WORD
He	is	my *friend*.	count noun
They	are	*students* from Japan.	....
These boxes	are	*some* of them.	....
Canada	is	a beautiful *country*.	....
This old hat	used to be	*John's*.	....
My grandmother	is	a little old *lady* with white hair.	....
George Moore	wasn't	*anyone* famous.	....
I	will be	an *engineering* student.	....

- Below are noun phrases that function as **direct objects** after transitive verbs. Underline the main word of the direct object and identify what type it is.

```
                            SENTENCE (S)
                           /            \
            NOUN PHRASE (NP) + VERB PHRASE (VP)
                SUBJECT            PREDICATE
                                   /        \
                       VERB (TRANSITIVE) + NOUN PHRASE (NP)
                                           DIRECT OBJECT          TYPE OF WORD
```

SUBJECT	VERB (TRANSITIVE)	DIRECT OBJECT	TYPE OF WORD
I	saw	John Brown.	name
We	needed	some money.	....
The Johnsons	are going to buy	a few.	....
Mr. Jones	heard	something strange.	....
We	liked	those two young ladies from Japan.	....
I	will get	another one.	....
Our neighbors	lost	everything.	....
John	wants	all of them.	....

EXERCISE 23.1 | Transitive Verb + Direct Object; Verb *BE* + Complement. See page 57.
EXERCISE 23.2 | Summary Exercise: Practice with Determiners. See page 57.

EXERCISES FOR SECTIONS 1-4

Exercises for Section 1
EXERCISE 2.1 | Count and Mass Nouns

Use a mass noun + *is* **or a plural count noun +** *are* **to fill the blank spaces.**

Examples: (lemon)   *Lemons are* yellow.
                (food)   *Food is* expensive.

(furniture)   1. .... expensive.
(car)   2. .... useful.
(rice)   3. .... grown in Asia.
(tool)   4. .... important.
(lime)   5. .... sour.
(chalk)   6. .... not always white.
(knife)   7. .... sharp.
(sugar)   8. .... sweet.
(wool)   9. .... used for making clothing.
(flower)   10. .... beautiful.
(butter)   11. .... a dairy product.
(research)   12. .... important.

EXERCISE 2.2 | Containers and Units of Measure Used with Mass Nouns

A. Fill in blanks with the proper form of a word from the list. In a few blanks, more than one word can be used.

    bar   gallon   piece
    bottle   glass   slice
    bowl   head   tube
    bunch   loaf   stalk
    cup   pair   bag

1. Would you like another .... of meat?
2. She bought a .... of celery and a .... of lettuce.
3. Mother baked two .... of bread, a .... of white and a .... of rye. For dinner, we each had several ....
4. I need a new .... of shoes.
5. For lunch I always eat a .... of soup and drink a .... of milk.
6. When you go downtown, get me a .... of toothpaste.
7. At the filling station I got ten .... of gas.
8. Mr. Johnson owns a nice .... of land.

9. Mrs. Palmer asked Mary to get two .... of grapes and a .... of cabbage when she went to the grocery store.
10. We don't have any soap in the house. When you go to the store, get two ....
11. Will you buy me a .... of red ink when you go shopping?
12. Please have another .... of tea.

B. Answer the questions in accordance with the container, the unit of measure, or the quantity in the picture.

1. Do we have to get any paper towels?
2. Did you buy very many potatoes?
3. Do we have a bunch of celery?
4. Can I bring some wine?
5. Is toothpaste on sale this week?
6. Shall I get any bread?
7. What did Henry pick at the orchard?
8. Shall I get some lettuce for the salad?
9. Do you need more eggs?
10. Is he taking any beans on the camping trip?
11. How much mustard do we have?
12. How much yogurt does Sue eat every day?
13. Did you buy any milk?
14. What's in this bag?
15. Why did we run out of soda at the party?

EXERCISE 3.1 | Words Used as Both Count and Mass Nouns

Which of the italicized nouns are count and which are mass?

1. There isn't any *room* left for a signature.
   There isn't any *room* in the hotel large enough for our meeting.
2. *Exercise* in the outdoors will do you a lot of good.
   This *exercise* about mass and count nouns isn't too hard, I hope.
3. The word "bank" is used most frequently in the *sense* of "financial institution."
   When I heard what she's done, I said to myself "What was the *sense* of that?"
4. The *light* over the sink just went out.
   The *light* on the horizon must be the dawn.
5. This plywood isn't the *thickness* I ordered.
   The *thickness* of the fog slowed down traffic.
6. Their *performance* has already been postponed twice.
   The *performance* of that engine has been outstanding.
7. His *union* was asking for a pay raise.
   The *union* of the two parties wasn't finally achieved until 1932.
8. The red hot *iron* is then rolled into sheets in the rolling mill.
   When Sue finished ironing, she put her hot *iron* right on the tablecloth.
9. My *weight* hasn't increased for some time.
   The two-pound *weight* wasn't enough to balance the scale.
10. When Mr. Cross died, he left his *business* to his oldest son.
    We'll have to consult an expert about this *business* of language training.

EXERCISE 4.1 | Identifying Noun Modifiers

A. Underline the adjectives, nouns, and noun possessives which are used as *noun modifiers* in these sentences. Do not underline the noun that is modified by them.

1. Four stone lions guard the ancient bridge.
2. The rich blue color reminded me of the beautiful Caribbean.
3. In this Mexican town you can see Canby's tomb.
4. This exterior latex paint is recommended for wood surfaces.
5. The mosque's tile floors were made many years ago.
6. From the nearby hills you can enjoy a delightful aerial view of the city.
7. This museum houses a magnificent collection of the king's treasures.
8. Several boring papers deal with Homer's poetry.
9. The newest Columbia University catalogue will be sent to you very soon.
10. A few Spanish landowners have large farms in the valley.

B. Substitute a modifier from the following lists for each underlined word of Part A. Rewrite the sentences.

ADJECTIVES		NOUNS	NOUN POSSESSIVES
big	interesting	marble	Charlemagne's
deep	lovely	metal	church's
excellent	marvelous	oil	emperor's
French	overall	plaster	Pushkin's
green	latest	mail order	
historic	foreign		
high	small		

EXERCISE 6.1 | Definite and Indefinite Articles

Fill *a, an* or *the* in the blanks.

1. Grandfather was .... kind man with .... heart as large as life.
2. Clarence Spicer was .... man who invented .... universal joint for automobiles.
3. My uncle made .... fortune for himself in .... Canadian paper industry.
4. She was involved in .... couple of scandals in .... first year of her career.
5. .... present economic situation came about as .... result of overinvesting.
6. I had .... disagreement with .... friend of mine recently.
7. .... family must now earn two and a half times what they earned in .... 1960's.
8. We were talking about .... coming Christmas holidays.
9. .... difference seems unimportant, but I think it shows how much confusion is common at .... present time.
10. In .... appendix of this book .... author has provided seventeen dialogs.

EXERCISE 6.2 | Definite and Indefinite Determiners

Write a list of things you saw when you came to class, or things in the room you are in now. Include examples of singular and plural count nouns, using them in both definite and indefinite noun phrases.

Examples: DEFINITE: the door, two windows, the tall tree on the corner, the salesman at the store, those students at the table, etc.

INDEFINITE: a bicycle, some cars, houses, windows, a dog, some books, an open door, etc.

EXERCISE 7.1 | Identifying Noun Phrases

Identify the noun phrases. First underline the noun phrases in these sentences. Then below the line identify each word of the noun phrase: Name, Mass noun, Count noun, Determiner, Noun possessive, Number, Adjective, Premodifying noun. Study the model.

Model: <u>Canada</u> is <u>a beautiful country</u>.
           NAME   DET. ADJ.   COUNT N.

1. Dexter made two mistakes.
2. No passengers were lawyers.
3. Bill's wife likes fur coats.
4. The Parkers prefer fresh milk.
5. Grape jelly is on sale today.
6. Mr. Fields ate some stale bread.
7. The two girls poured out the chicken soup.
8. Betty's baby brother caught a cold.

Exercises for Section 2

EXERCISE 8.1 | Prepositional Phrases Used as NP Modifiers

A. Write these sentences again, adding a prepositional phrase as a modifier of the subject of the sentence. You may use one of the suggested prepositions or another one.

Example: The little girl looked very pretty. { with / on / near }

           The little girl with long red hair looked very pretty.

1. A woman asked me to hold her books. { at / next to / in }

2. Everybody had a good time. { with / at / in }

3. The planes made a lot of noise. { from / by / above }

4. Our lunch was excellent. { after / during / before }

5. Somebody lost his hat. { with / from / on }

6. Nothing was appreciated. { from / by / of }

7. People have great interest in it. { of / from / with }

8. Our vacation was a marvelous one. { during / in / at }

B. Write three sentences of your own using a prepositional phrase to modify an NP used as the direct object of a transitive verb.

EXERCISE 9.1 | Practice with Pronouns
Rewrite each sentence, substituting personal pronouns for the italicized noun phrases.

Example: *Alice's* lunch money is in *Jack's* desk.
Her lunch money is in *his* desk.

1. *The toy* doesn't belong to *this girl*.
2. *One of the boys* left early to get *a ticket*. (He or One of them)
3. *That* is *my sister's* radio.
4. Please come with *my uncle and me*. *He and I* are going to his teacher's house for dinner.
5. *Mr. Gray and Mr. Beck* shouldn't pay *Tom* for only two week's work.
6. These aren't *Bob's* books. They belong to *you and me*.
7. There's room in *Jack's and my* office for *the desk*.
8. *Mary* is *my parent's* friend's daughter.

EXERCISE 11.1 | Noun Determiners Indicating Great and Little Quantity
Complete the sentences with one of these determiners. In some sentences more than one is possible.

little	few	a little
a few	much	many
a lot of	lots of	a little bit of
a great deal of	a good deal	

1. That's an old story. I've heard it .... times.
2. I don't think we'll need .... corn flour.
3. What was he getting at? I couldn't make .... sense out of what he said.
4. He gets .... exercise on the tennis courts.
5. Although most of them have gone south, ... birds will stay all winter.
6. Jimmy got .... baking powder on his suit.

7. Paul doesn't like sports and he has .... interest in the sports reports on TV.
8. Most of us thought Conrad would win the election. .... people gave Wilson a chance.

EXERCISE 11.2 | Summary Exercise: Noun Determiners
Fill the blanks with appropriate noun determiners.

I'd like to drive .... car through .... capital city of France. There are .... beautiful things to see. .... traveler would enjoy seeing ....famous Champs Elysees, ... Arch de Triomphe, and .... Eiffel Tower. There are .... interesting old buildings, too.

After seeing Paris, I'd drive through .... pretty little towns. I'd stop at .... little store and buy .... wine, ... bread, and .... cheese. I'd stop .... car on .... mountainside, and look down at .... little town while I ate .... picnic lunch.

EXERCISE 12.1 | Practice with Possessive Pronouns
Complete the sentences with a possessive pronoun: *hers, his, mine, ours, theirs, yours.*
1. I used my birthday money to buy a dictionary, but my brother got an ice cream maker with ....
2. We're offering free samples to everyone. Come in and pick .... up today.
3. Although they have a larger restaurant, we think .... serves better food.
4. Mrs. Blue has an excellent hair dryer, but I just can't get .... to work.
5. Trudy makes the best custard in the world. None is as smooth as ....
6. We sold our house for $45,000, but our neighbors got $55,000 for ....

EXERCISE 12.2 | Noun Substitutes
Form a logical second sentence using the suggested noun substitute as the sentence subject.
Model: We can get oranges in the store all winter. Most...
              Most come from Florida.
         (or) Most are shipped by truck.
1. Your razor is no good. This one...
2. Seven of the eggs are brown. Five...
3. A lot of people wanted to get tickets. Some...
4. Henry spilled the salad dressing. A little bit...
5. Mr. Jones doesn't go to New Year's parties. That...
6. Many things determine success or failure. A good deal...
7. She left the peas cooking on the stove. A few...
8. The children used all the butter on their toast. None...

EXERCISE 13.1 | Summary Exercise: Practice with Pronouns

Fill the blanks with the correct form.

It was moving day at the Dawsons'. Everybody in the family had to help with the work.

Mrs. Dawson called .... *(hers, her)* husband, "Jim, where is .... *(my, mine)* hat box? I can't find .... *(she, her, it)*.

"It's in the truck, Ann," Jim said. "I'm going to get .... *(mine, my)* clothes now. I told Tommy to bring .... *(his, him)* clothes, too. Mary has already brought .... *(her, hers)*. .... *(She's, He's)* cleaning .... *(his, hers)* room."

"Good!" said Ann. "We'll all want some lunch soon. Tommy and Mary can go out and get some hamburgers. .... *(Those, They)* can eat .... *(his, theirs)* at the restaurant and bring .... *(ours, our)* back here."

"I could eat .... *(my, mine)* right now, but it's only ten o'clock," said Jim. I'm hungry. I'm hungry enough to eat .... *(your, yours)*, too!"

"Well," laughed Ann, "why don't you go out and get the hamburgers now and bring .... *(they, them, it)* back? Then all of .... *(them, us, we)* can eat when we want to."

"Good idea! I thought you'd never think of .... *(its, it)!*"

EXERCISE 13.2 | Summary Exercise: Practice with Noun Determiners and Noun Substitutes

Complete the sentences with one of the words in parentheses.

1. I'll see you in .... days. *(a few, a lot, few)*
2. .... children were studying. They were mostly interested in watching the football game. *(a few, a lot, few)*
3. .... birds were bathing, but .... were eating seeds. *(a few, a lot, few)*
4. I know .... people in Ottawa, but I don't know .... in Montreal. *(any, some)*
5. There weren't .... teachers at the party. but there were .... nurses. *(many, some)*
6. We don't have .... blue ink to color the map. We're asking for .... *(enough, more)*
7. She needs .... milk for her baby. She only has .... for two bottles. *(enough, more)*
8. Maxwell stayed in Japan. .... was his plan all along. *(that, that one)*
9. Art looked first in the top drawer. He thought the forks were in .... *(that, that one)*
10. You have to take your watch to the fifth floor for repair service. We don't do .... here. *(that, that one)*
11. Ann brought .... lunch along, but Katharine didn't bring .... *(her, hers)*
12. June was surprised to see Sarah's house because .... isn't as big. *(her, hers)*
13. .... packages were broken but not .... cereal was spoiled. *(many, much)*
14. We heard .... noise in the kitchen but couldn't see .... *(much, a lot of)*

48 GRAMMAR AND DRILLBOOK

Exercises for Section 3

EXERCISE 14.1 | Word Order

Use the words at the left in the correct order in the sentence.

Example: three / white / comfortable — We bought *three comfortable white* chairs.

1. colorful / a / new — She was wearing .... dress.
2. big / seven / red — I bought .... tomatoes.
3. those / rusty / old — .... tools are mine.
4. blue / new / whose — .... car is that?
5. pink / delicious / that — I'd like some more of .... grapefruit.
6. new / beautiful / white — We saw a .... ship.

EXERCISE 14.2 | Adjective Precedence with Origin Modifiers

Fill the blanks with the words at the left, being sure to use them in the proper order.

1. a / beautiful / Dutch / old — It's .... painting.
2. excellent / an / new / English — I bought .... dictionary.
3. Spanish / interesting / an / old — I met .... gentleman.

4. marvelous / old / some / French } He served us .... wine.

5. a / Japanese / famous / young } He's a .... architect.

6. interesting / Italian / an / new } She learned to make .... dish.

EXERCISE 16.1 | Definite and Indefinite Noun Substitutes

Fill the blanks with *another (one), others, the other (one)* or *the others*.

1. I found one of my shoes, but I couldn't find ....
2. There was one lamp on the table and .... on the desk.
3. There are two pieces of cake left. You take one and I'll eat ....
4. These glasses are dirty. Don't you have any ....?
5. The candy's all gone! There were six pieces. I ate one, but who ate ....?
6. My car's wearing out. I'm afraid I'll have to buy ....
7. There are three restaurants in town. Two of them are quite good, but .... is terrible!
8. Mr. Jones lost his job last month. He's trying to find ....
9. Mrs. Failor invited sixteen people for dinner at 7:00. At 7:30 only twelve people had come. She said to her husband, "Should we wait for ....?"
10. Mr. White was shopping for shirts at a department store. He said to the clerk, "I don't like these shirts. Are there any .... on sale?"

EXERCISE 16.2 | Definite and Indefinite Noun Substitutes

Revise the sentences, using *another, others, the other* or *the others* an noun substitutes.

Examples: Where are the other people?
Where are *the others*?

Another bus is coming.
Another is coming.

1. The other women couldn't come.
2. May I use the other glasses?
3. The other table is too small.
4. There are other cups in the kitchen.
5. Let's take another picture.

6. Other people were listening.
7. Do you have other dresses?
8. There's another meeting at 2:00.
9. The other radio doesn't work.
10. Do you have other suits that are cheaper?

EXERCISE 16.3 | Determiners and Noun Substitutes

Make up a sequel to these sentences. Use *one* of the words or expressions in parentheses in your sentence.

Example: One of the twins is a doctor in the Celebes now. *(another one, the other one)*
 The other one is a petroleum engineer in Alaska.
 (or) I don't know anything about the other one.

1. One of my uncles is a businessman and owns four gas stations. *(another one, the other one)*
2. One tire of Joe's car was flat. *(others, the others)*
3. I only need the heel replaced on one shoe. *(another, the other)*
4. Miss Stott forgot to order typewriter ribbons last week. *(no, none)*
5. The American Indians originally got all their horses from the Europeans. *(no, not...any)*
6. My favorite cities are San Francisco and Paris. *(either, other)*
7. Stan has two extra pencils. *(either, neither)*
8. Both of my brothers are in Greenland. *(either one, neither one)*
9. Jane spilled her tea on the floor. *(something, everything)*
10. The top drawer is empty. *(nothing, anything)*
11. Hastings is our most successful salesman. *(no one, everyone)*
12. We saw the door was open when we got back home. *(anyone, someone)*

EXERCISE 17.1 | Indefinite Pronouns

Repeat the sentences, substituting appropriate indefinite pronouns from the list in each.

anyone	anybody	anything
someone	somebody	something
no one	nobody	nothing

Example: Does { anyone / anybody / someone / somebody / no one / nobody } know the answer to the question?

1. I'll never say .... about it.
2. Neither of the boys would invite .... to the dance.

3. .... else came.
4. He'll have .... to say about it.
5. She knew .... at the party.
6. I think it's .... else's turn.
7. We didn't expect .... exciting to happen.
8. There's .... in that room.

EXERCISE 17.2 | Indefinite Pronouns + *else*

Take the part of Speaker B. Respond to Speaker A's statement with an indefinite pronoun + *else*. Follow the models. Notice the stress patterns.

	SPEAKER A	SPEAKER B
Models:	Joe ate the potáto salad.	Did he eat anything élse?
	Jóe ate the potato salad.	Did anyone élse eat it?

1. Vegetarians eat végetables.
2. My uncle has written a book about díalects.
3. I've stopped buying that bránd.
4. Blueberries are sold in pint báskets.
5. Janie wanted to make a píe.
6. Mr. Prátt enjoyed the first assignment.
7. We met George Bárr last night.
8. Jímmy gobbled a hamburger down quickly.

EXERCISE 18.1 | Identifying Noun Phrases

Identify the noun phrases. First underline the noun phrases in these sentences. Then below the line identify the parts of each noun phrase: Name, Mass noun, Count noun, Determiner, Adjective, Premodifying noun, Prepositional phrase, Indefinite pronoun, Noun substitute. Study the model.

Model: How many <u>good</u> <u>French</u> <u>restaurants</u> do <u>you</u> know?
                        ADJ. ADJ.   COUNT N.   PRON.

1. Most stores don't have either.
2. Several other students caught bad colds in the head.
3. Each one got something else.
4. Every door on our block has the same number of windows.
5. Did anyone you know make these delicious little green pickles?
6. I think the manager is the one in the blue coat.
7. Most are mine, but three are John's.
8. Anita can tell you a great deal about citrus fruits.

Exercises for Section 4

EXERCISE 19.1 | *All* and *all the* + NP

If it is possible, delete *the* from *all the* so the sentence will have a universal meaning (that is, it will be true in every situation). If the sentence can not have a universal meaning, then use *not all* + NP.

Examples: All the cats have four legs.
   All cats have four legs.   (true everywhere)
   All the dentists take care of people's teeth.
   All dentists take care of people's teeth.   (true everywhere)
   All the clothes are made of cotton.
   Not all clothes are made of cotton.   (not true of all clothes)

1. All the plants need water.
2. All the grass needs to be cut.
3. All the dogs are able to run.
4. I think all the boys should have a good education.
5. All the people need time to play as well as work.
6. All the houses have windows.
7. All the people sleep on beds.
8. All the children should be cared for.
9. It's important for all the workers to have the right kinds of food for good health.
10. All the young children swim well.
11. All the men work in an office.
12. All the boys get very good grades on math tests.

EXERCISE 19.2 | Summary Exercise: Practice with Noun Determiners

Fill the blank space with one of the two words in parentheses.

Example: (much, many)   I don't have *much* money.

(a little, a few)   1. We bought .... vegetables from the farmer.
(a little, a few)   2. Did you get cream? Yes, we got ....
(some, any)   3. The waiter didn't bring us .... bread.
(some, any)   4. I said I didn't want ....
(both, all)   5. The two boys were running to school. .... were late.
(either, neither)   6. He wouldn't tell his father or his mother. He would tell .... of them.
(either, neither)   7. Would you prefer coffee or tea? .... one will be all right.
(much, many)   8. I don't make a lot of money. John doesn't make .... either.
(a great deal, a great deal of)   9. Do you have much time? No, I don't have ....

(another, other)	10.	Would you like .... piece of cheese?
(no, none)	11.	Jack Jones raises vegetables, but he has .... for sale.
(a lot of, much)	12.	Betty bought .... candy, but her mother wouldn't let her eat it.
(much, enough)	13.	Would you like some more soup? Yes, please, but don't give me ....
(each, every)	14.	The ladies .... baked a cake.
(no one, anyone)	15.	There wasn't .... at the door.
(all, every)	16.	Billy broke the pencils. He broke .... of them.
(all, every)	17.	.... children like to play games.
(it, them)	18.	Some of the furniture was expensive. Some of .... was cheap.
(another, the other)	19.	I lost two books. I found one of them, but I can't find ....
(every, every one)	20.	The apples were large, and .... had a beautiful red color.

EXERCISE 20.1 | Summary Exercise: Practice with Determiners and Predeterminers
Complete the sentences using appropriate mass nouns or count nouns.

1. All the .... are pleased about the invitations.
2. Every one of the .... was prepared.
3. Both the .... gave money to their sister.
4. None of the .... ever arrived for the people's use.
5. A few of the .... wanted free tickets.
6. All the .... was used for his education.
7. Both .... and .... are leaving now.
8. All .... can breathe and move about.
9. One of the .... walked home with her.
10. Each .... asked for a glass.
11. It was planned for both ....

EXERCISE 20.2 | Practice with Predeterminers

Write ten sentences using items from Columns (1), (2) *and* (3). Use other nouns if you wish.

Examples: *Both of my sisters* are nurses.
Do you know *either of those men?*
Every one of the chairs was taken.

(1) PREDETERMINERS	(2) ARTICLE **THE,** DEMONSTRATIVES, AND POSSESSIVE PRONOUNS	(3) NOUNS	
a little of	the	sisters	candy
a few of	this	water	ice cream
some of	that	gifts	boys, girls
every one of	these	books	men, women
each one of	those	paper	rice
many of	my	money	water
much of	your	sugar	cheese
either of	his	chairs	
neither of	her	potatoes	
all of	our	food	
both of	their	trees	
several of		food	

EXERCISE 20.3 | Substitute Forms after Predeterminers

Rewrite the sentences using *it, them,* a demonstrative, or a possessive pronoun to replace the noun phrase that occurs after the predeterminer.

Examples: I haven't seen either of *the boys.*
I haven't seen either of *them.*

Try some of *my ice cream.*
Try some of *it.*
(or) Try some of *mine.*

1. Much of the food was spoiled.
2. I'd like a few of those apples.
3. Many of the potatoes in the ground were frozen.
4. Some of his toys were broken.
5. All of her money was taken.
6. You may have either of these pencils.
7. Both of our children are grown.
8. Neither of their wives could come.

9. You can use a little of my toothpaste.
10. Every one of the women liked to gossip.
11. They didn't use any of his research.
12. Each one of the students received a book.

EXERCISE 22.1 | Position of Origin Modifiers

Take the part of Speaker B. Add the origin modifier to the noun phrase in the correct position. Follow the model.

SPEAKER A: That attractive young actress is Swedish.
SPEAKER B: Oh, really? I like attractive young Swedish actresses.

1. A: This fine linen is Irish.
   B: Oh, really? I like ....
2. A: Kim's green jade bracelet is Burmese.
   B: Oh, really? I like ....
3. A: This old pink vase is Italian.
   B: Oh, really? I like ....
4. A: Her beautiful new skirt is French.
   B: Oh, really? I'd like to see her ....
5. A: This long red sausage is German.
   B: Oh, really? I've never seen a ....
6. A: That old stone axe is Indian.
   B: Oh, really? I've never seen an ....
7. A: Those small white trucks are Japanese.
   B: Oh, really? I've heard about those ....
8. A: That rich brown coffee is Colombian.
   B: Oh, really? I've heard about that ....
9. A: Our convenient new office is downtown.
   B: Oh, really? I've heard about your ....
10. A: His big new ranch is in Texas.
    B: Oh, really? I've heard about his ....

EXERCISE 23.1 | Transitive Verb + Direct Object; Verb *BE* + Complement

A. Write seven sentences using a noun phrase as the direct object of a transitive verb. Supply your own subject, but use verbs and noun phrases from the lists below.

Example: Mr. and Mrs. Jones *invited*   *several guests.*

VERBS (TRANS)	DIRECT OBJECT (NP'S)
liked	several guests
invited	a fine student
is	all the food
sold	engineers
are	Mrs. Jones
was	their house
met	Tom's grandmother
were	some groceries
bought	artists
am	nurses
ate	his bicycle
lost	one of my shoes
heard	the flowers
brought	the money
saw	something
found	a good artist
wanted	somebody important
enjoyed	very important people
broke	the music

B. Write five sentences using a noun phrase as complement after one of the forms of the verb *BE*. Use noun phrases from the list above.

Example: Jack's a fine student.

C. Write six sentences of your own, using a noun phrase as the direct object of a transitive verb, and as the complement after the verb *BE*.

EXERCISE 23.2 | Summary Exercise: Practice with Determiners

Read the paragraphs, selecting the correct determiner to fill each blank.

   We visited .... *(an, a)* language school the .... *(other, another)* day. There was .... *(a lot of, many)* activity in the building. We saw .... *(a little, a few)* teachers near .... *(this, the)* office. .... *(Many, Much)* students were walking in the halls. A .... *(great deal of, great many of)* them were from .... *(a, the)* Middle East, but .... *(others, another)* were from South American countries.

   We stopped to talk to two girls. .... *(Neither, Either)* the younger girl .... *(nor, or)* the older .... *(one, ones)* could speak English well. They .... *(all, both)* tried very hard and .... *(all the, all)* four of us enjoyed .... *(their, our)* conversation.

We visited .... *(a, the)* class, too. There were only .... *(a little, a few)* students in .... *(a, the)* class. The students .... *(each, every)* had .... *(many, much)* opportunities to speak English.

We had only .... *(a little, a few)* more time after class. My friend saw two teachers in .... *(another, other)* classroom, and we wanted to speak to .... *(them, those)*. .... *(Mine, My)* friend was sure that .... *(either, neither)* would be glad to tell us .... *(most, more)* about .... *(a, the)* school.

We had to leave at noon, but we plan to go back .... *(another, the other)* time soon.

SECTION 5

Sentences as Objects of Transitive Verbs
Direct Speech
Indirect Speech
Indirect Speech—Verb Forms and Tenses
Indirect Speech—Choice of Tenses

24 Sentences as Objects of Transitive Verbs

- In previous lessons we learned that a noun phrase (NP) may be used as the direct object of a transitive verb. In this and the next few grammar sections we shall be using *complete sentences* as the objects of transitive verbs. We shall study these in connection with *direct* and *indirect speech*.

- These are examples of sentences with verb phrases that consist of a transitive verb plus an *NP* used as direct object.

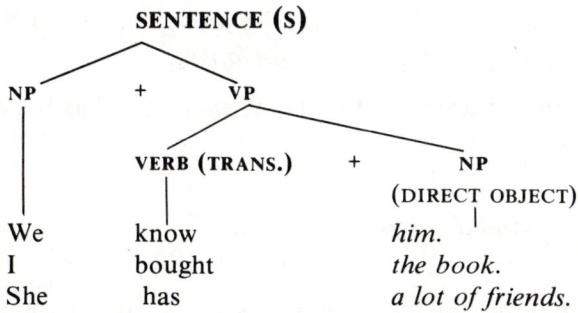

- These are examples of sentences with verb phrases that consist of a transitive verb plus a *complete sentence* used as direct object.

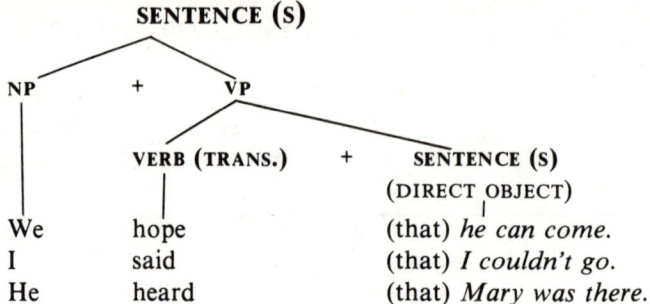

In the examples above, *he can come, I couldn't go* and *Mary was there* are complete sentences used as the objects of the verbs *hope, said* and *heard*.

- The word **that,** which precedes the sentences used as objects, is called a *subordinator* or *subordinating conjunction*. It is shown in parenthesis (that) because its use is optional.

  The use of *that* shows that the sentence which follows is a subordinate or dependent part of the main sentence. *That + Sentence* is called a **clause**. It is a *subordinate clause*.

  Clauses which are used in the same manner as NPs (as subjects, objects of verbs or prepositions, etc.) are traditionally called *noun clauses*.

- The following are three more examples of *that + Sentence* used as the direct object of a transitive verb.

    I know *that he's coming.*
    She said *that she wanted to come with us.*
    They told me *that they could speak Finnish.*

The subordinator *that* may be deleted with no difference in meaning. The three examples below mean exactly the same as the ones above.

    I know *he's coming.*
    She said *she wanted to come with us.*
    They told me *they could speak Finnish.*

> ## PRACTICE
>
> **A. Delete** *that*.
>
> 1. He said that he was coming.
>   *He said he was coming.*
> 2. Did she tell you that I should go?
>   *Did she tell you I should go?*
> 3. He told me that I should study Japanese.
>   ....
> 4. Did they say that they could speak English?
>   ....
> 5. When did they say that they were coming?
>   ....
>
> **B. Use** *that*.
>
> 1. Did he say he knew you?
>   *Did he say that he knew you?*
> 2. When did they say they could come?
>   ....
> 3. Why did Bill say he wasn't going?
>   ....
> 4. Helen said she was giving a party.
>   ....
> 5. I told him I'd be glad to help.
>   ....

EXERCISE 24.1 | Identifying Direct Objects of Transitive Verbs. See page 86.

EXERCISE 24.2 | Omission of the Subordinator *that*. See page 86.

Extra Drill 24.1

25 Direct Speech

- By **direct speech** we mean the words that a speaker actually uses when he says something. In writing, we indicate that someone is speaking by using quotation marks ("..."). Note in the examples below that statement quotations (*"I can't come tomorrow."*) are set off by commas from reporting tags *(John said)*. Notice that reporting tags can be placed in several positions:

> "I can't come tomorrow," *John said.*
> *Mary said,* "I'll be here early."
> "Come in the kitchen," *her mother said,* "and finish your soup."

- Questions that a speaker asks are also put into quotation marks. Note the location of the question mark.

    She asked, "Can I come, too?"
    "Would you like to come in?" *Mrs. Jones asked her guests.*

- When the reporting tag occurs in the middle or at the end of the quotation its verb may precede its subject NP.

    "Mary is ill," *reported John.* (or *John reported.*)
    "Are you going to join us, dear," *asked his wife*, "or will you stay here?"

EXERCISE 25.1 | Punctuation of Direct Speech. See page 87.

Extra Drill 25.1

26 Indirect Speech

- Often a person reports what someone else has said or thought without using his exact words. We call this **indirect speech**. Indirect speech is often called *indirect quotation* or *reported speech*.

- Let us suppose you are with John and Mary and you hear them say:

    JOHN: "I have to study."
    MARY: "I'm going to the movies."

    John and Mary have used *direct speech*. If you report what they are saying, using *indirect speech* you could say:

    John says that he has to study.
    Mary says she's going to the movies.

- To make it clear whether a person is using direct or indirect speech in these lessons, we shall use the two words **speaker** and **reporter**. The *speaker* is the one who uses direct speech. The *reporter* is the person who uses indirect speech to report what the speaker has said. For example:

    JOHN (SPEAKER):   "I need my book."
    HENRY (REPORTER):   John says he needs his book.

    MARY (SPEAKER):   "I can't find my hat."
    HELEN (REPORTER):   Mary says she can't find her hat.

- When reporting what someone else has said, it is necessary to make various changes in the direct speech. For example, when a speaker refers to himself, he uses the pronoun *I, my, me,* etc. When the reporter tells what this person says, he refers to the speaker as *you, he* or *she* and uses the other appropriate pronoun forms (*him, her,* etc.).

    The subordinator *that* can be used or omitted.

PRACTICE

1. John says, "I need my book."
   John says he needs his book.
2. Mary says "I have no money."
   Mary says that she has no money.
3. Jim says, "That book isn't mine."
   ....
4. Mrs. White says, "I can't speak Spanish."
   ....
5. Helen says, "English is my native language."
   ....
6. Mr. Brown says, "I've never been to Paris."
   ....
7. June says, "Bill's coming to see me."
   ....
8. Mr. and Mrs. White say, "We can't come to dinner."
   ....

Extra Drill 26.1

- *Say* and *tell* are the two verbs that are most commonly used with indirect speech. Both may be followed by *(that)* + Sentence.

Say and *tell*, however, belong to two different classes of transitive verbs. The verb *tell* must be followed by an *indirect object*. In these examples *me* and *Mr. Wilson* are the indirect objects.

> He told *me* that he'd come.
> We told *Mr. Wilson* we'd help him.

The verb *say* may be followed directly by *(that)* + Sentence. It may also be followed by an indirect object preceded by *to*.

> She said that she'd come.
> She said *to me* that she'd come.

Say and *tell* also function this way in direct speech:

> She said, "I'll be there."
> She told me, "I'll be there."
> She said to me, "I'll come."

EXERCISE 26.1 | The Verbs *say* and *tell*. See page 88.
EXERCISE 26.2 | Indirect Speech. See page 88.

- In reporting direct speech, it is usually necessary to make changes in these three elements: (1) *verb forms and tenses*, (2) *pronouns*, (3) *adverbials of time and place*. It is also sometimes necessary to change the word order and to use a subordinator. These things are discussed in the following pages.

27 Indirect Speech: Verb Forms and Tenses

- When a person reports something that someone else said, he is usually talking about a conversation that took place at a past time. It is usual, then, for the reporter to begin his sentence by saying something like, *He said that...*, *Mary told me*, *Mr. White thought...*, etc. The verb that is used in this part of the sentence is called the *main verb*.

    The use of a past tense main verb usually requires a change in verb tense in the direct speech verb.

- If the *speaker* uses a *present* tense form in his direct speech, the *reporter* generally uses the *past* tense when reporting.

BILL (SPEAKER):	"I'm late."
JIM (REPORTER):	Bill *told* me he *was* late.
TOM (SPEAKER):	"I *don't want* to go."
HENRY (REPORTER):	Tom *said* he *didn't want* to go.

    Extra Drill 27.1

- The speaker may use a modal in his direct speech. (The modals are: *can/could, may/might, shall/should, will/would, ought to* and *must*.)

    After a past tense main verb the modals are usually changed as follows: *can* → *could*; *will* → *would*; *may* → *might*.

BOB (SPEAKER):	"I'll *help* you."
TED (REPORTER):	Bob said he *would help* me. (or he'd *help*)
JIM (SPEAKER):	"I *can't hear* the teacher."
TOM (REPORTER):	Jim said he *couldn't hear* the teacher.
MR. BROWN (SPEAKER):	"I *may buy* a small car next time."
MR. WHITE (REPORTER):	Mr. Brown said he *might buy* a small car next time.

    If "may" is used to express permission, "could" is often used in the reported speech.

MOTHER (SPEAKER):	"You *may invite* Barbara, Mary."
MARY (REPORTER):	Mother told me I *could (might) invite* Barbara.

- There is no change in the form of the modals *could, should, would* and *ought to* to show past tense.

    MRS. BROWN (SPEAKER):   "I *should work* in my garden."
    MRS. WHITE (REPORTER):   Mrs. Brown said she *should work* in her garden.

The modal *must* has no past tense. To express the idea of *must* in the past, it is necessary to use *had to*.

                                                         Extra Drill 27.2-3

    MR. JOHNSON (SPEAKER):   "I *must leave* at noon."
    MR. GREEN (REPORTER):   Mr. Johnson told me he *had to leave* at noon.

PRACTICE

SPEAKER	REPORTER *(Use pronouns)*
1. John said, "I'm late." What did he say?	He said he was late.
2. Henry says, "I'll be glad to help you, Dick." What did he tell Dick?	He told him he'd be glad to help him.
3. Bob says, "I can't find my hat." What did he say?	....
4. Mr. Brown says, "I must get a haircut." What did he say?	....
5. Mary says, "I'm sorry I won't be able to go with you, John." What did she tell John?	....
6. Mrs. Green says, "I should go to the grocery store." What did she say?	....
7. Mrs. White says, "You may go, Mary." What did she tell Mary?	....
8. Helen says "I won't tell anyone else." What did she say?	....

- If the *speaker* uses a *past tense* form in his direct speech, the *reporter* often has the choice of using either the *past tense* or the *past perfect* (*had* + past participle) when reporting.

    JANE (SPEAKER):   "I wrote the letter."
    MAE (REPORTER):   Jane told me that she *wrote (had written)* the letter.

> ## PRACTICE
>
> **Step 1:** Practice this conversation.
>
>   (1) MARY: I saw you downtown.
>   (2) JOHN: I didn't see you.
>   (3) MARY: I saw you from the window of the bus.
>   (4) JOHN: I bought myself a suit.
>   (5) MARY: I like your new suit.
>
> **Step 2:** Bob reports the conversation (above) that he has heard between John and Mary. *Repeat.*
>
>   (1) BOB: Mary said she had seen John downtown.
>   (2) BOB: John said he hadn't seen her.
>   (3) BOB: Mary said she saw him from the window of the bus.
>   (4) BOB: John said he bought himself a suit.
>   (5) BOB: Mary said she liked his new suit.
>
> **Step 3:** The student now takes the part of John. John reports the conversation he has had with Mary.
>
>   (1) JOHN: Mary said she saw me downtown.
>   (2) JOHN: I said ....
>   (3) JOHN: ....
>   (4) JOHN: ....
>   (5) JOHN: ....

- If a *speaker* uses the *present perfect* (*have/has* + past participle), the *reporter* will generally use the *past perfect* (*had* + past participle) when reporting what was said.

    TOM (SPEAKER):   "*I've quit* my job." *(have quit)*
    DICK (REPORTER):   Tom told me he*'d quit* his job. *(had quit)*

    BOB (SPEAKER):   "I *haven't finished* my work yet."
    JIM (REPORTER):   Bob said that he *hadn't finished* his work yet.

EXERCISE 27.1 | Direct and Indirect Speech. See page 89.

> **Extra Drill 27.4**

28 Indirect Speech: Choice of Tenses

- We have seen that present tense verbs in direct speech are usually changed to past tense in indirect speech.

    MR. BATES (SPEAKER): "I *have* a meeting."
    MR. CANDY (REPORTER): Mr. Bates *said* he *had* a meeting.

However, the reporter may often choose to use the present tense in his reported speech. If the speaker's information is still true when it is reported, or if the information is still of interest, the reporter may use the *present tense*. Study these examples:

    CARLOS (SPEAKER): "My native language is Spanish."
    JOHN (REPORTER): Carlos *said* his native language *is* Spanish.

When John reported Carlos' speech, it was still true that Carlos' native language is Spanish. John, therefore, can use the present tense.

Here is another example:

    MR. FRANK (SPEAKER): "There *are* a lot of mountains in my country."
    MR. FOLGER (REPORTER): Mr. Frank *said* there *are* a lot of mountains in his country.

It is still true that there are a lot of mountains there, so the present tense can be used in the subordinate clause when reporting.

> **Extra Drill 28.1**

- When the *present perfect* is used in direct speech, it is usually changed to the *past perfect* in reporting speech.

    TOM (SPEAKER): "I *haven't told* anyone."
    BOB (REPORTER): Tom told me he *hadn't told* anyone.

If the action or event described by the speaker still continues to have an effect or is still relevant at the time of reporting, then the reporter will probably use the *present perfect* in his indirect speech.

    MR. KELLY (SPEAKER): "I've *been* a mechanic for 16 years."
    MR. JONES (REPORTER): Mr. Kelly said that he's *been* a mechanic for 16 years.

Since Mr. Kelly is still a mechanic at the time of Mr. Jones' report, Mr. Jones uses the present perfect.

EXERCISE 28.1 | Choice of Tenses in Indirect Speech. See page 89.

> **Extra Drill 28.2**

SECTION 6

Question Words
Indirect Questions: Question-word Questions

29 *Wh*-Question Words and Transformations

- The question words *who, whom, whose, what* and *which* are often used like noun substitutes and are called *nominal question words* or **Wh-question words.**

- *Who, whom* and *whose* ask questions about people. When *who* is used as the subject of a sentence it always takes a singular verb.

    Who *wants* an orange?
    Who *speaks* Spanish?

- When used with the verb *BE, who* is the complement. The true subject follows the verb *BE* and determines whether the verb is singular or plural.

    Who *is he?*
    Who *are they?*

- Both *who* and *whom* can be used as the direct object of a transitive verb. *Who* is used in informal speech; *whom* is used in formal language.

    Who did you see?   (informal)
    Whom did you see?   (formal)

The following table shows the uses of *who* and *whom:*

WHO AS SUBJECT, OBJECT AND COMPLEMENT

SUBJECT	VERB	OBJECT
Who	called	me?
Who	wanted	it?

COMPLEMENT	VERB	SUBJECT
Who	is	he?
Who	are	they?

OBJECT	AUXILIARY	SUBJECT	VERB
Who	did	you	tell?
Whom	did	they	see?

- In informal language, *who* is used as the object of a preposition. The preposition always comes at the end of the question.

  Who did you give the book *to?*

  Whom is used in formal language as the object of a preposition. Two forms of the sentence are possible when *whom* and a preposition are used. The second is more formal than the first.

  (1) *Whom* did you give the book *to?*
  (2) *To whom* did you give the book?

> **PRACTICE**
>
> **Change these formal questions to informal ones.**
>
> **Example:** To whom did you give the book?
> *Who did you give the book to?*
>
> 1. Whom did they see?
> ....
> 2. For whom did he buy the gift?
> ....
> 3. To whom did you wish to speak?
> ....
> 4. Whom did you meet there?
> ....
> 5. About whom was he talking?
> ....

EXERCISE 29.1 | Using *who* and *whom*. See page 91.

- Question-word questions (or *Wh*-questions) can be thought of as being formed by a process of **transformation.** That is, one type of sentence is *transformed* into another by some grammatical means.

  In this *Wh-question transformation,* a *Wh*-question word substitutes for an NP in the basic sentence.

  Who (whom) substitutes for an NP and asks about the identity of a person. **What** asks the identity of things, including abstractions such as occupation and nationality.

  > That's *John.*   *Someone's* calling.   He's *an engineer.*
  > *Who's* that?   *Who's* calling?   *What* is he?

  A double arrow (⇒) is used to show that a construction results from the process of transformation.

  > She saw *someone.*   ⇒ *Who(m)* did she see?
  > She bought *a dress.*   ⇒ *What* did she buy?
  > *Something* happened. ⇒ *What* happened?

- **Whose** substitutes for possessives. *Whose* can be used with or without a following NP.

  > That's *Tom*'s.   ⇒ *Whose* is that?
  > That's *his car.*   ⇒ *Whose (car)* is that?

- **Which** may be followed by an NP, by the substitute word *one*, or it may be used alone.

  I want *that pencil*. ⇒ { *Which pencil* do you want?
  Which one do you want?
  Which do you want? }   **Extra Drill 29.1**

  Which indicates selection from a list of limited possibilities. *What* indicates selection from an almost unlimited list.

  Which finger got hurt?
  What country are you from?

- *When, where, how* and *why* are *adverbial Wh*-question words.

  In the *Wh*-transformation, they have these meanings:

  when asks about time, (*now, last week, in the morning, soon,* etc.)

  He's coming *tomorrow*.   *When*'s he coming?

  where asks about place and direction, (*here, there, on the corner, downtown,* etc.)

  He's going *to Japan*.   *Where*'s he going?

  how asks about manner and health, (*fast, slowly, by plane, with a great deal of care,* etc.)

  He's coming *by car*.   *How*'s he coming?
  She doesn't feel *well*.   *How* does she feel?

  why asks about reason or purpose, (*because of the rain, to see his aunt,* etc.)

  She's running *because she's late*.   *Why*'s she running?

PRACTICE

Transform the sentences to *Wh*-questions. Use the appropriate question word to replace the italicized word or words.

Examples:

He's going *to school* today.   ⇒ Where's he going today?
He's going to school *today*.   ⇒ When's he going to school?

1. They're going *by car*.   ⇒ ....
2. He came home *because he was tired*.   ⇒ ....
3. His office is *downtown*.   ⇒ ....
4. She's coming *next week*.   ⇒ ....
5. He met her *in Mexico*.   ⇒ ....

Extra Drill 29.2

- *How* + adverb (*how often, how far, how long*) replaces a corresponding adverbial which expresses *frequency (sometimes, every week)*, *distance* (*two miles, a long way*, etc.), or *time duration* (*a long time, several weeks*, etc.).

It's *a long way* to Troy.	⟹ *How far* is it to Troy?
He comes *every week*.	⟹ *How often* does he come?
He's been here *a long while*.	⟹ *How long* has he been here?

- *How much* and *how many* are the forms for quantity expressions.

He wants *several books*.	⟹ *How many* (books) does he want?
He needs *five dollars*.	⟹ *How much* (money) does he need?

- *How* + adjective (*how tall, how wide, how high, how hot,* etc.) replaces an expression of degree.

It's twelve stories high.	⟹ *How high* is it?

EXERCISE 29.2 | *Wh*-Questions. See page 91.

Extra Drill 29.3

30 Indirect Questions: *Wh*-Questions

- Questions that are reported using indirect speech are called *indirect questions*.

- The two principal types of questions in English are called (1) question-word questions (or *Wh*-questions), and (2) Yes/No questions. These two types of questions are not reported in indirect speech in the same way. Let us look first at type (1), *Wh-questions*.

- When using indirect speech to report *Wh*-questions, the original question becomes a clause used as the direct object of a main verb. The subject and verb of the clause are always used in *statement word order;* that is, *the subject comes before the verb,* and the auxiliary *do* is omitted. Study these examples:

JOHN (SPEAKER):	"Who *was he?*"
TED (REPORTER):	John asked who *he was.*
MARY (SPEAKER):	"Which one *did he want?*"
JANE (REPORTER):	Mary asked which one *he wanted.*
JIM (SPEAKER):	"When *are they coming,* Alan?"
ALAN (REPORTER):	Jim asked me when *they were coming.*

In reporting questions, as in reporting statements, it is usually necessary to make changes in verb forms, pronouns and adverbs.

PRACTICE

	SPEAKER	REPORTER
A.	These are questions that John asked.	
	1. "What time is it?" *What did he ask?*	He asked what time it was.
	2. "When are they leaving?" *What did he ask?*	....
	3. "How can I help?" *What did he ask?*	....
B.	These are questions that Mary asked.	
	1. "Where's my English book?" *What did she ask?*	....
	2. "Who will speak Spanish with me?" *What did she ask?*	....
	3. "Which movie did they see?" *What did she ask?*	....

EXERCISE 30.1 | Reporting Question-word Questions. See page 92.

Extra Drill 30.1-5

- Sentences with this kind of clause are also used in answer to question-word questions. Such clauses are commonly called *included questions* or **embedded questions.** In these clauses, the subject always precedes the verb.

  QUESTION: Who *is he?*
  ANSWER: I don't know who *he is.*

  QUESTION: Where's *Mrs. Hoffman?*
  ANSWER: I don't know where *she is.*

  QUESTION: What *did your friends say?*
  ANSWER: I don't remember what *they said.*

- Remember that in some questions, the question-word is the subject of the verb. In the clause, of course, the question word as subject comes before the verb and usually takes strong stress for contrastive emphasis.

  QUESTION: *Who told you that?*
  ANSWER: I don't remember *who told* me that.

  QUESTION: *What happened to John?*
  ANSWER: I haven't heard *what happened* to him.

PRACTICE

Substitute progressively.

SUBJECT	MAIN VERB	CLAUSE
John	knows	when it happened.

TEACHER	STUDENT
Past Tense	John knew when it happened.
remember	John remembered ....
where	....
Bob	....
Yes/No Question	....
how	....
Negative Statement	....
why	....
know	....
nobody	....
hear	Nobody heard why it happened.

EXERCISE 30.2| Embedded Questions. See page 93.
EXERCISE 30.3| Embedded Questions. See page 93.

Extra Drill 30.6-7

SECTION 7

Indirect Questions: Yes/No Questions
Indirect Speech: With Imperatives

31 Indirect Questions: Yes/No Questions

- In reporting *Yes/No questions,* the subordinators **if** and **whether** are used. There is no difference in meaning. As usual, the subject comes before the verb in the clause and the verb tense is changed.

HENRY (SPEAKER):	"Can John go?"
BOB (REPORTER):	Henry asked *if* John could go.
(or)	Henry asked *whether* John could go.
MARY (SPEAKER):	"Did you tell anyone, Jane?"
JANE (REPORTER):	Mary asked me *whether* I told anyone.
(or)	Mary asked me *if* I told anyone.

PRACTICE

A. Use *if* in the indirect questions.
1. "Did Mary come, Helen?" Jim asked.
   Jim asked Helen if Mary came.
2. "Can you hear me, John?" Miss Brown asked.
   ....
3. "Are your friends going?" Bob asked Tom.
   ....
4. "Do you speak English, Pedro?" Jane asked.
   ....

B. Use *whether* in the indirect questions.
1. "Are your parents coming, Helen?" Jane asked.
   ....
2. "Will you help me?" Mrs. White asked her son.
   ....
3. "Must you leave, Mrs. White?" Mrs. Johnson asked.
   ....
4. "Will you stay for dinner, Mr. Failor?" Mrs. White asked.
   ....

EXERCISE 31.1 | Indirect Speech: Yes/No Questions. See page 93.

> Extra Drill 31.1-3

- The words **or not** are frequently used with *whether* and sometimes with *if*. They are added at the end of the clause and make no difference in meaning.

    JOHN (SPEAKER): Is Bill coming?
    BOB (REPORTER): John asked me *whether* Bill was coming *or not*.
    (or) John asked me *if* Bill was coming *or not*.

It is also possible to use *whether or not* as a connected phrase. (This cannot be done with *if*.)

    JOHN (SPEAKER): "Is Bill coming?"
    BOB (REPORTER): John asked me *whether or not* Bill was coming.

PRACTICE

A. Use *whether... or not*.

1. "Did you see the movie, June?" Tom asked.
   Tom asked June whether she saw the movie or not.
2. "Do you have a radio, Tom?" Bob asked.
   ....
3. "Can you swim, Ted?" Bob asked.
   ....
4. "Do you believe me?" Mary asked June.
   ....

B. Use *if... or not*.

1. "Did you pass the exam?" Mr. White asked his son.
   Mr. White asked his son if he passed the exam or not.
2. "Can you go, Bob?" Jane asked.
   ....
3. "Do you have any homework, Bill?" his father asked.
   ....
4. "Do we have enough time?" Mr. Jones asked me.
   ....

C. Use *whether or not*

1. "Must you leave?" Mrs. White asked me.
   Mrs. White asked me whether or not I had to leave.
2. "Would you like to go? Tom asked me.
   ....
3. "Do you speak English, Mario?" I asked.
   ....
4. "Will you help me, Bob?" Ted asked.
   ....

EXERCISE 31.2| Indirect Speech: with *whether...or not*. See page 94.

Extra Drill 31.4-6

- Sentences containing clauses introduced by the subordinators *if* and *whether* are not used solely to report questions.

Clauses with *if* and *whether* (which derive from Yes/No questions) are commonly used after the *negative* and *interrogative* forms of *remember, know, learn, hear, see* and some other verbs.

> Do you know *whether* she can come?
> I can't remember *if* I told him *or not*.
> We weren't sure *whether* we were going the right way *or not*.

In *affirmative* statements, *if*- and *whether*-clauses commonly occur after the verb *wonder*.

> I wonder if I can do it.
> We wonder whether we should go or not.

PRACTICE

A. Use *if*. Begin each sentence with *I wonder*.

1. Did I turn off the light?
   I wonder if I turned off the light.
2. Is my English fluent enough?
   ....
3. Am I on time?
   ....
4. Should I go?
   ....
5. Can I find the hotel again?
   ....

B. Use *whether*.

1. Does he speak Japanese?
   I wonder whether he speaks Japanese.
2. Does this radio work?
   ....
3. Was that Mr. Wilson?
   ....
4. Will she know me?
   ....
5. Is it going to rain again?
   ....

EXERCISE 31.3| Embedded Questions. See page 94.

EXERCISE 31.4| Indirect Speech. See page 95.

EXERCISE 31.5| Summary Exercise: Direct and Indirect Speech. See page 95.

32 Indirect Speech With Imperatives

- An **imperative** is a request or command. Imperatives are formed by using the base form of the verb with no subject expressed.

    Come here.   Sit down.   Listen to me.

    Negative commands use *don't*.

    Don't sit down.   Don't worry.   Don't tell anyone.

    Commands may be addressed to a particular person or persons using an NP at the beginning or end of the command.

    Come here, John.   Everyone listen to me.
    Be quiet, children.   Jim, come with me.
    Don't do that, Bill.   Children, sit down.

- An affirmative imperative is reported in indirect speech by using an infinitive (*to* + base form of the verb).

    ALAN (SPEAKER):   "Call me tonight, Jim."
    JIM (REPORTER):   Alan asked me *to call* him tonight.

    MRS. BROWN (SPEAKER): "Help me, Mary."
    JOHN (REPORTER):   Mrs. Brown asked Mary *to help* her.

    Negative imperatives are reported by using the word *not* before the infinitive.

    TEACHER (SPEAKER):   "Don't sit down, children."
    JOHN (REPORTER):   The teacher told the children *not to sit down*.

    MR. WHITE (SPEAKER): "Don't worry about it, Helen."
    HELEN (REPORTER):   Mr. White told me *not to worry* about it.

- Imperatives that are requests use "ask" as the reporting verb. Commands use "tell." Compare the two sets of examples above.

- The word "please" is frequently omitted in the indirect imperative, but it can appear within the infinitive. With negative requests *please not* is used within the infinitive.

    Please leave your shoes outside.
    He asked us *to please leave* our shoes outside.

    Please don't hang up yet.
    She asked me *to please not hang up* yet.

PRACTICE

                                                                REPORTER

A. **What did Mr. Fuller tell his students?**
   1. "Repeat after me."   He told them to repeat after him.
   2. "Practice every chance you get."   ....
   3. "Don't worry about making a few mistakes." ....
   4. "Listen to the radio."   ....
   5. "Don't forget to listen to tapes every day." ....

B. **What did Mrs. Brown tell her son?**
   1. "Come home early."   She told him to come home early.
   2. "Don't stay out late."   ....
   3. "Go to the drugstore for me on the way home." ....
   4. "Help your sister with her Spanish before you go to bed." ....
   5. "Call your father and tell him that dinner is on the table." ....
   6. "Don't forget to set your alarm."   ....

EXERCISE 32.1 | Indirect Speech with Imperatives. See page 96.
EXERCISE 32.2 | Summary Exercise: Indirect Speech. See page 97.
EXERCISE 32.3 | Summary Exercise: Direct and Indirect Speech. See page 97.

Extra Drill 32.1-3

SECTION 8

Indirect Speech: Pronoun Forms
Indirect Speech: Adverbials of Time and Place; Verbs "come/go" and "bring/take"

33 Indirect Speech: Pronoun Forms

- We have noted in previous lessons the fact that in reporting direct speech, it is necessary to change pronoun forms. That is, if a woman speaker says "I," "my," etc., the reporter must use "she," "her," and other appropriate forms.

- Choosing the correct pronoun when a speaker uses "you," "we," and "they," sometimes causes difficulty. These are points to remember:

  (a) If the speaker uses *you (your, yours)*:

  If the speaker uses the pronoun *you* to refer to the person reporting the conversation, the reporter uses *I, me, my* or *mine*.

      Mary said to Jim, "I saw you downtown."
      Jim (reporter):   Mary said she saw *me* downtown.

  If it is clear that the speaker is using *you* as a plural form, then the reporter uses *we, us, our,* or *ours*.

      Mary said to Jim and his sister, "I saw *you* downtown."
      Jim (reporter):   Mary said she saw *us* downtown.

  > **Extra Drill 33.1**

PRACTICE

	SITUATION	REPORTER
1.	Bob says to you, "Are they good friends of yours?"	Bob asked me if they were good friends of mine.
2.	Tom says to you and your brother, "What time did you arrive?"	Tom asked us what time we arrived.
3.	Jim says to you and your friend, "Are the books yours?"	....
4.	Mr. White says to you, "Which book is yours?"	....
5.	Jane says to you and your friends, "Can you come to my party?"	....
6.	The teacher says to you and your classmates, "Do I have all your compositions?"	....
7.	Ted says to you, "Who are you taking to the dance?"	....

(b) If the speaker uses *we (us, our, ours):*

If the speaker does not include the reporter when he says *we,* then the reporter uses *they (them, their, theirs).*

Jim says to Bill, "*We*'re late."
Bob (reporter):   Jim says *they*'re late.

If the speaker includes the reporter when he says *we,* then the reporter uses *we (us, our, ours).*

Jim says to Bill and Bob, "*We*'re late."
Bob (reporter):   Jim says *we*'re late.

Extra Drill 33.2

> ## PRACTICE
>
> In this Practice, Bob is the reporter. Use pronoun forms for the indirect object and the subject of the clause.
>
> | | SITUATION | BOB (REPORTER) |
> |---|---|---|
> | 1. | Jim says to Bob and Bill, "Do we have enough money?" | Jim asked us if we had enough money. |
> | 2. | Helen says to Tom and Jane, "What should we do?" | Helen asked them what they should do. |
> | 3. | Mr. Black says to his wife, "Must we go?" | .... |
> | 4. | Jane said to Ted and Bob, "Will we have to hurry?" | .... |
> | 5. | Ted said to George and Henry, "Is that our car?" | .... |
> | 6. | Tom said to Ed and Bob, "What time do we have to be there?" | .... |

EXERCISE 33.1 | Pronouns *we* and *they* in Indirect Speech. See page 100.

- If a speech is reported to someone mentioned in the direct speech, the *he, she, they,* or *you* of direct speech is changed to *you.*

> Fuller says of Jones: I hope he (Jones) is ready by six a.m.
> Smith reports to Jones: Fuller said he hopes *you*'re ready by six a.m.

34 Indirect Speech: Adverbials of Time and Place; Verbs *come/go* and *bring/take*

- *Adverbials of time* include such words as *today, tomorrow, now, then,* and such expressions as *last year, in the morning,* etc. *Adverbials of place* are such words as *here, there,* and expressions such as *at the office, on the corner,* etc.

- When you report what someone else has said, you must use time and place words that are correct for the time when you are reporting and the place where you are reporting from. Let us take an example:

> *Mr. Failor and Mr. Johnson are talking together in Mr. Johnson's home. It is Tuesday evening.*
>
> MR. JOHNSON: I hope you can have lunch with us tomorrow.
>
> MR. FAILOR: I'd like to very much.

MR. JOHNSON: Why don't you come to my office first? I want you to meet Mr. White. We'll go to lunch from there.

MR. FAILOR: All right. **I'll meet you there at noon tomorrow.**

Now it is 11:00 a.m. on Wednesday, the next day. Mr. Johnson and Mr. White are talking.

MR. JOHNSON: Mr. Failor is coming for lunch. I'd like you to meet him and go to lunch with us.

MR. WHITE: Fine. I'd like that. What time will we go?

MR. JOHNSON: **Mr. Failor said he'd meet us here at noon today.**

Compare Mr. Failor's direct speech, and Mr. Johnson's report of what he said:

MR. FAILOR (SPEAKER): I'll meet you *there* at noon *tomorrow*.

MR. JOHNSON (REPORTER): Mr. Failor said he'd meet us *here* at noon *today*.

Mr. Johnson had to change the adverb of place *there* to *here* because he was in his office when he reported the speech. Note also that it was necessary for him to change the time word *tomorrow* to *today*.

PRACTICE

Choose the correct time word or expression in parentheses. The time words in brackets above the name of the speaker indicate the time or day when the speaker made a statement, and the time when it is being reported.

Example:

[Tuesday]
MARY: "I can't go tonight."

[Wednesday]
REPORTER: Mary said she couldn't go *last night*. (tonight, last night)

1. [Monday]
   BILL: "I'm leaving tomorrow."

   [Tuesday]
   REPORTER: Bill said he's leaving ………. (tomorrow, today)

2. [Wednesday]
   MRS. BROWN: "I bought some nice oranges yesterday."

   [Thursday]
   REPORTER: Mrs. Brown said she bought some nice oranges ………. (yesterday, day before yesterday)

3. [Tuesday]
   MR. GREEN: "The meeting is next week."
   [Wednesday]
   REPORTER: Mr. Green said the meeting is .... *(this week, next week, week after next)*

4. [1970]
   MRS. WHITE: "I visited Paris three years ago."
   [1971]
   REPORTER: Mrs. White said she visited Paris .... *(2 years ago, 3 years ago, 4 years ago)*

5. [1:00 p.m. Tuesday]
   MR. JONES: "I'll see you there at 4:00 this afternoon."
   [3:00 p.m. Tuesday]
   REPORTER: Mr. Jones said he'd see us here .... *(an hour ago, in an hour)*

6. [Sunday]
   MRS. LONG: "I'm leaving for Japan the day after tomorrow.
   [Tuesday]
   REPORTER: Mrs. Long told me she's leaving for Japan .... *(today, tomorrow, the day after tomorrow)*

7. [11:00 a.m. Friday]
   MR. SHORT: "I saw Ted a few minutes ago."
   [4:00 p.m. Friday]
   REPORTER: Mr. Short said he saw Ted .... *(a few minutes ago, at noon, this morning)*

- When reporting someone else's speech, a reporter often has a choice of several different ways of expressing the adverbials of time and place used by the speaker.

    There is no one simple rule to be followed. Often, however, (depending, of course, on the location of the speaker and reporter) the adverb *here* will be reported as *there*, or *there* as *here*. Also, the demonstratives *this* and *these* are often changed to *that* and *those*.

    The time adverb *now* is commonly replaced by *then*. *Today* is often reported as a particular day (*Tuesday, Wednesday,* etc.) or frequently as *that day*. *Tomorrow*, also, is commonly reported as a particular day of the week (*Thursday, Friday,* etc.) or as *the next day* or *the following day*.

    Extra Drill 34.1-3

- Certain verbs which indicate direction also are changed. The most common such verbs are *come* and *bring* (which denote direction toward the speaker) changing to *go* and *take* (which denote direction away from the speaker), and vice versa.

PRACTICE

Mr. Markley has taken his son Steve to lunch at the Parrot Restaurant for the first time. Mr. Markley is speaking.

"This is my favorite restaurant."

"I always come here."

"I'm sure you'll like the food here."

"I've wanted to bring you here for a long time."

"Waiter, will you bring us some coffee, please."

That night Steve reports to his mother what his father said. Choose the correct word to complete his statements.

Dad said .... *(this, that)* was his favorite restaurant.

He told me he always .... *(comes, goes)* .... *(here, there)*.

He said he was sure I'd like the food .... *(here, there)*.

He said he had wanted to .... *(bring, take)* me .... *(here, there)* for a long time.

Then he asked the waiter to .... *(bring, take)* us some coffee.

EXERCISE 34.1 | Indirect Speech: Adverbials of Time and Place. See page 101.

EXERCISE 34.2 | Summary Exercise: Practice in Reporting Speech. See page 103.

Extra Drill 34.4

SECTION EIGHT 85

EXERCISES FOR SECTIONS 5-8

Exercises for Section 5

EXERCISE 24.1 | Identifying Direct Objects of Transitive Verbs

Underline the direct object of the verb. Tell whether it is a noun phrase (NP) or a sentence (S).

Examples: I saw <u>him</u>. (NP)
  When did he tell you <u>he was coming</u>? (S)

1. Have you seen Mary?
2. They told me that they didn't know.
3. She said she wanted to come with us.
4. Some big boy hit that little boy in the green sweater.
5. Does he speak English?
6. Helen's giving a party.
7. I know I can't do it.
8. He bought a marvelous old Dutch painting.
9. I don't often see him.
10. He thinks he'll be able to come.

EXERCISE 24.2 | Omission of the Subordinator *that*

Take the part of Speaker B. Answer Speaker A's question using the correct information. Omit the subordinator "that." Study the model.

Model: *I'm going to Switzerland.*
SPEAKER A: Did Mr. Forbes say that he was going to Spain?
SPEAKER B: No, he said he was going to Switzerland.

1. *I'm taking Lisa to Joe's Diner.*
   A: Did Gordon say that he was taking Lisa to the Palace Restaurant?
   B: No, ...
2. *I listen to tapes every chance I get.*
   A: Did you say that you never listen to tapes?
   B: No, ...
3. *I want you to come to the dance.*
   A: Did you say that you wanted me to stay home?
   B: No, ...
4. *I want to become a famous chef.*
   A: Did Bill Sykes say that he wanted to be a doctor?
   B: No, ...

5. *I'm going to take a vacation in March.*
   A: Did Emily say that she was going to the regional conference in March?
   B: No, ...

6. *Doris doesn't know about it.*
   A: Did Art tell you that Doris knew what happened?
   B: No, ...

7. *Neil rides the bus to work with Cindy.*
   A: Did Art tell you that Neil drove Cindy to work?
   B: No, ...

8. *The cat's choking on a bone.*
   A: Did your sister tell you that the cat was choking on a string?
   B: No, ...

9. *Gordon dreams about clam chowder quite often.*
   A: Did your sister tell you that Gordon ate clam chowder quite often.
   B: No, ...

10. *Jerry is nibbling the cheese.*
    A: Did the clerk tell Jane that Jerry was gobbling the cheese?
    B: No, ...

EXERCISE 25.1 | Punctuation of Direct Speech

Punctuate these sentences, following the examples that are given.

Examples: (1) She said I can't go tonight.
               She said, "I can't go tonight."

               (2) I can't go tonight she said.
               "I can't go tonight," she said.

               (3) He asked me when can you come?
               He asked me, "When can you come?"

               (4) Where are you going? they asked.
               "Where are you going?" they asked.

1. He said I don't know how to dance.
2. Can you come to my party? she wanted to know.
3. We're late I said and we're going to miss the bus.
4. Where are we going? I asked.
5. He asked in a low voice who's that girl over there?
6. That's Margaret I answered.
7. Why can't we come? the children asked.
8. I want to tell you something June said to Anne.
9. What time are you going I asked and when will you come back?
10. How did man learn to write? the professor asked.

EXERCISE 26.1 | The Verbs *say* and *tell*

Fill the blanks with an appropriate form of *say* or *tell*.
1. What did you ....?
2. The doctor .... his nurse to hurry.
3. You didn't .... him, did you?
4. "Why can't you .... me?" I wanted to know.
5. "I don't like you," Barbara .... to John.
6. "Who ....that?" I asked.
7. What did you .... him?
8. I didn't .... them anything.
9. "Who .... you that?" I asked.
10. I .... everyone to come.
11. I .... "Everybody come."
12. Did I understand you to .... he's a famous Japanese astronomer?
13. John came over to me and ...., "Let's go."
14. Barbara .... to Tom, "You're rude!"
15. Why did she .... that to him?

EXERCISE 26.2 | Indirect Speech

Use *indirect speech* to report the statements made below. Use the past tense in all your reported sentences. Use *that* or omit it.

Example: John said, "I want to go, too."
John said he wanted to go, too.
John said that he wanted to go, too.

1. Mrs. Wilde said, "I'm fluent in Spanish and French."
2. Mary said, "I practice all the time."
3. Mr. Forest said, "I asked Bill to wash my new car."
4. Helen said, "Jim wants to meet my friend June."
5. Tom said, "I always invite them to my parties."
6. Milly said, "I'm trying to turn off the water in the kitchen."
7. Mrs. Collins said, "I'm going to Canada."
8. Mr. Johnson said, "Someone is waving a white handkerchief."
9. Mike said, "I don't like cafeterias."
10. Janet said. "It's printed in the appendix."

EXERCISE 27.1 | Direct and Indirect Speech

Change the indirect statements to direct speech, paying close attention to the punctuation. Change the direct speech verbs to present tense.

Example: John said he wouldn't tell Bill.
John said, "I won't tell Bill."

1. I said I wanted to go.
2. Jane said she was very anxious to come.
3. Bill said he would tell us all about it.
4. Barbara said she was engaged to be married.
5. Mr. Wells said he had to stop smoking.
6. Mrs. Forest said she couldn't find her son.
7. I said I didn't want to miss it for anything.
8. Jackie said she might study Arabic.

EXERCISE 28.1 | Choice of Tenses in Indirect Speech

Report the statement made in the first picture. Use a past tense verb where the situation has changed, but do not change the tense when the situation has not changed.

Example 1:

"Baked Halibut is on special."   *He said that baked halibut is on special.*

Example 2:

"Oyster cocktail is on special."   *He said that oyster cocktail was on special.*

"The cook's still working on your order."

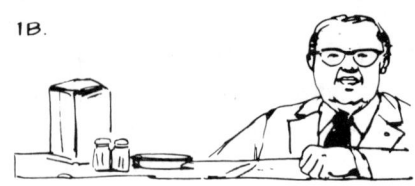

She said that . . . .

"Mrs. Chang owns the restaurant."

He said that . . . .

"Miss Stott is out for a minute."

He said that . . . .

"They've sent him to a tropical country."

She said that . . . .

"He's studying prehistoric pottery."

She said that . . . .

"I'm not going to eat that cake."

She said that . . . .

Exercises for Section 6

EXERCISE 29.1 | Using *who* and *whom*

Rewrite these informal statements and questions in more formal language, using *whom* whenever possible. Remember, *whom* can only be used as an *object* of the verb.

Examples: (1) Who did you give the book to? (2) Who's your friend?
Whom did you give the book to? *(No change;* Who *is not an object.)*
(*or*) To whom did you give the book?

1. Who did you send the letter to?
2. Who were they talking about?
3. Who told you to come?
4. Who did you tell?
5. Do you know who's coming?
6. Tell me who was at the party.
7. Who did you dance with?
8. Can you remember who you told?
9. Who are you giving the watch to?
10. Who did you see at the dance?

EXERCISE 29.2 | Forming Wh- Questions

Student A: Change the sentence to a Wh-question, replacing the italicized words by the corresponding question word.

Student B: Answer the question with a short answer.

	STUDENT A	STUDENT B
EXAMPLES:		
They went *downtown*.	*Where did they go?*	*Downtown.*
No one called.	*Who called?*	*No one.*

1. He's leaving *at ten o'clock*.
2. John's coming *by plane*.
3. *Dr. Smith* will take care of her.
4. The ruler is *twelve inches long*.
5. He comes *frequently*.
6. He was crying *because he fell down*.
7. It's *two miles* to the next village.
8. *Carol's* going to study Arabic.
9. They're going to stay *for two weeks*.
10. They're going *by boat*.
11. That's *John's* book.
12. That suit is *fifty dollars*.
13. He met *someone* in Brazil.
14. The room was *twenty feet wide*.
15. Those are *Helen's* books.

EXERCISE 30.1 | Reporting Question-word Questions

Use indirect speech to report these question-word questions. Use past tense.

Example: "Where did you go?" Tom asked Mary.
Tom asked Mary where she went.

1. "Where do you live?" Tom asked Charles.
2. "What should I do?" Mary asked her mother.
3. Mr. White asked Mr. Smith, "When did you see Mr. Black?"
4. "How did you meet Miss Wu?" Bob asked Jim.
5. "Why must I invite Barbara?" Helen asked her mother.
6. "How can Tom go?" Mary asked.

Continue the exercise using these pictures.

92 GRAMMAR AND DRILLBOOK

EXERCISE 30.2| Embedded Questions

Answer the questions. Begin your answers with "I don't know." Use pronouns as the subject of the clause.

Example: Where's Mrs. Hoffman?
              I don't know where she is.

1. Who's that man?
2. Whose book is this?
3. Why can't Dr. Wilson go?
4. How many languages does Dr. Ferguson speak?
5. What did the policeman say?
6. When does the lecture begin?
7. Where are Mr. and Mrs. Johnson?
8. How long are your friends going to stay?
9. What time does the play start?
10. Where's Miss Wu from?

EXERCISE 30.3| Embedded Questions

Complete each sentence with a clause beginning with a question word from list A, B and C.

A. Use *who, whom* or *which*.
B. Use *when, what, why* or *how*.
C. Use *how* + adverb (*how far*, etc.) or *how* + adjective (*how tall*).

1. I don't know ....
2. Do you remember ....
3. Can you tell me ....
4. I can't remember ....
5. I haven't heard ....
6. Have you heard ....

Exercises for Section 7

EXERCISE 31.1| Indirect Speech: Yes/No Questions

Report the following questions using indirect speech. Use either *if* or *whether* as the subordinator. Use past tense in you reported questions.

Examples: "Can you hear me, John?" the teacher asked.
               The teacher asked John if he could hear her.

               "Are they leaving?" he asked.
               He asked if they were leaving.

1. "Are they planning to go?" he wanted to know.
2. "Do you have to leave, Tom?" Jim asked.
3. "Are they engaged?" Mary asked.

4. "May we use the container?" they asked.
5. "Is the cheese from Denmark?" Mrs. Brown asked me.
6. "Do you know the answer, June?" the teacher asked.
7. "Did you solve the problem, Henry?" the teacher asked.
8. "Did Jane tell you that?" Bill asked Helen.
9. "Can you go, Mary?" I asked.
10. "Can Mary go?" I asked her mother.

EXERCISE 31.2 | Indirect Speech

A. Complete the sentences with a clause made from the words in parentheses. Use *whether...or not* in all your sentences.

1. The professor asked everyone *whether they were prepared for the examination or not.* (prepared/examination)
2. I asked the bus driver .... (had/change/dollar)
3. Dr. Hunter asked me .... (I/took/medicine/regularly)
4. I asked the druggist .... (drug/dangerous/heart)
5. I asked him .... (knew/that/Dr. Long/my friend)

B. Complete these sentences with a clause. Use *whether...or not* or *if...or not*.

1. The teacher asked the students ....
2. He asked me ....
3. We asked the doctor ....
4. Helen asked her friend ....
5. Everyone asked me ....

EXERCISE 31.3 | Embedded Questions

Complete these sentences with a clause derived from a Yes/No question. You may use *if, whether, whether or not, whether...or not,* or *if...or not* in completing your sentences.

Example: I wonder *whether I should take a raincoat or not.*

1. I wonder ....
2. I can't remember ....
3. Do you know ....
4. I haven't heard ....
5. Do you remember ....

EXERCISE 31.4| Using Indirect Speech

Speaker A asks a question which Speaker B does not hear or understand. Then Speaker A has to repeat the question using indirect speech and B then answers the question.

	SPEAKER A	SPEAKER B
Example:	Do you have any brother or sisters.	I'm sorry. I didn't understand you. Would you mind repeating that?
	I asked *if you had any brothers or sisters.*	*Oh, yes. I have two older brothers.* (or) *I just have one younger sister.*

1. Do you live around here?
2. Are you from this area?
3. Where were your parents born?
4. Do you enjoy winter sports?
5. What do you like to do on weekends?
6. Do you have a favorite movie star?
7. Do you want to go to a movie with me?
8. Can you type sixty words a minute?
9. Would you like to see my rock collection?
10. Do you have a rich uncle?

EXERCISE 31.5| Summary Exercise: Direct and Indirect Speech

Change the indirect questions to direct speech, paying close attention to the punctuation and verb tenses.

Examples: He asked me if I wanted to go.
He asked me, "Do you want to go?"

She asked what time it was.
She asked, "What time is it?"

1. They asked Bill where he was going.
2. She asked Carlos if he spoke English.
3. Mrs. Long asked her son if he would help her.
4. We asked them if they would go with us or not.
5. I asked whether there were many applicants.
6. He asked her whether or not she really wanted to go.
7. He asked who they were.
8. Helen asked her friend if she knew Tom.

EXERCISE 32.1 | Indirect Speech with Imperatives

Report these imperative sentences. Use "told" as the main verb in all your reported sentences. Use pronouns.

1. What did Bob's mother tell him?
   She told him not to worry.

2. What did the teacher tell the children?

3. What did they say to me?

4. What did she say to Henry?

5. What did the doctor tell Mr. Palmer?

6. What did Bob tell Margaret?

7. What did Tom say to his dog?

8. What did the teacher say to her students?

EXERCISE 32.2 | Summary Exercise: Indirect Speech

Report these statements, questions and imperatives, using the patterns for indirect speech. Use either *if* or *whether* as the subordinator in reporting Yes/No questions.

Examples: "Where's the party?" I asked.
I asked where the party was.

"Can you go, Tom?" I asked.
I asked Tom if he could go.

1. "Is Bill a good friend of yours, Bob?" I asked.
2. "Did you write your composition?" Tom asked Henry.
3. "Don't play in the street," the policeman said to the children.
4. "Have you heard the good news?" Mrs. Thompson asked me.
5. "You must hurry, Barbara," Mrs. Palmer said.
6. "Whose car is that?" Mr. Fama asked me.
7. "Which one do you want, Tom?" Bob asked.
8. "Don't run in front of the cars, Helen," Mrs. White said.
9. "A good deal of French is spoken in Canada," he said.
10. "Should I tell him?" Mrs. Brown asked me.
11. "You can't go out," Mr. Jones said to his son.
12. "I saw him last night," I said.
13. "Why did you do that?" Tom asked Henry.
14. "Do your homework, Tom." Mr. Brown said.
15. "I may not be able to go," they said.
16. "Where did you put my watch?" Steve asked his brother.

EXERCISE 32.3 | Summary Exercise: Direct and Indirect Speech

A. First describe the action that is taking place in the two pictures. Then reconstruct the direct speech that the speaker might be using in the first picture.

1.

Example: "Sit in that chair, Billy." *or* "Billy. Please sit down."

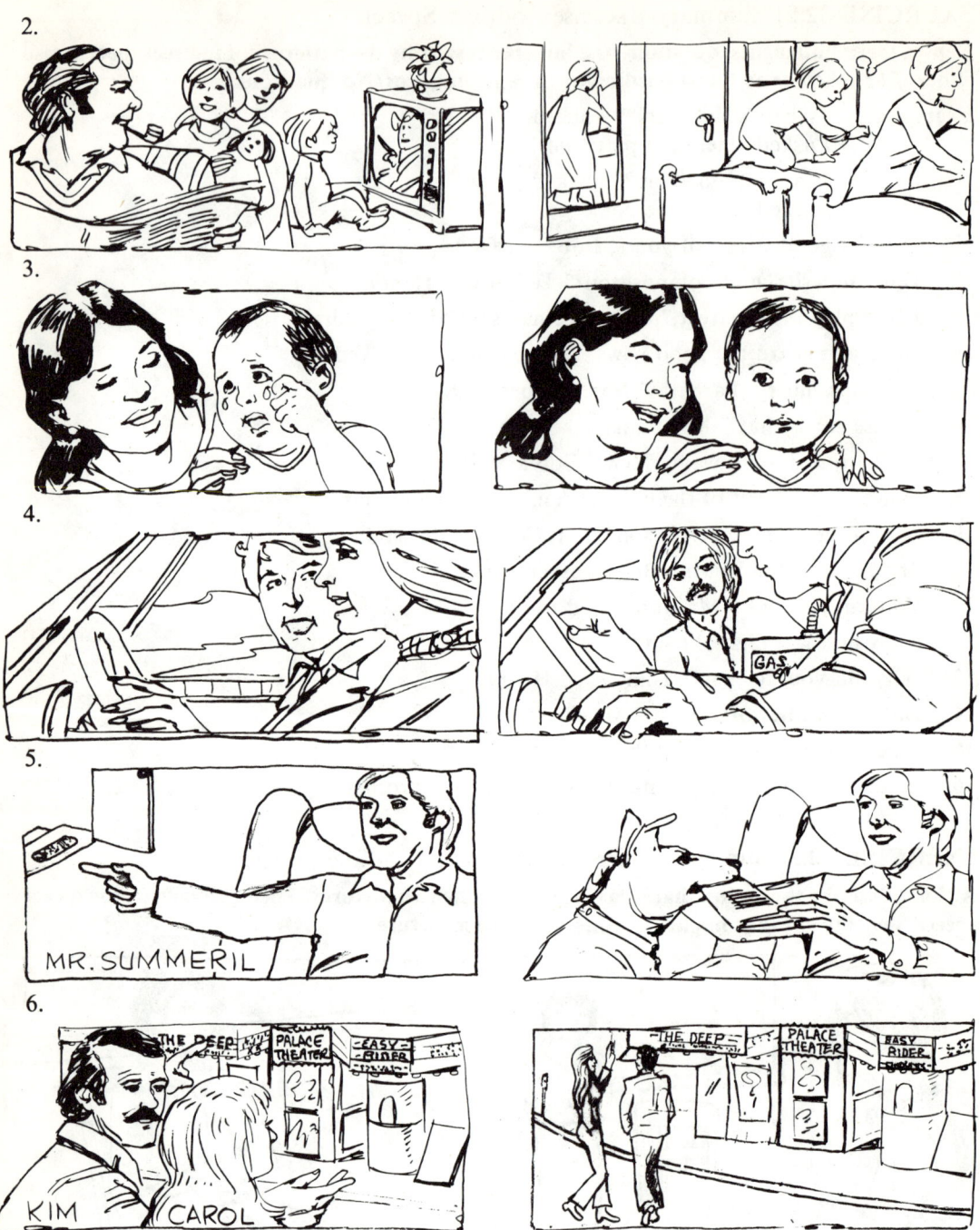

B. Now take the part of a reporter and report the direct speech with indirect speech.
Example: (Picture 1.) The teacher told Billy to sit in the chair (to sit down).

Exercises for Section 8

EXERCISE 33.1 | Pronouns *we* and *they* in Indirect Speech

A. Read this exercise.
   (1) MR. BROWN: We're going to be late.
   (2) MR. WHITE: It's only eleven o'clock.
   (3) MR. BROWN: Our meeting starts at eleven fifteen.
   (4) MR. WHITE: I have all our papers ready.
   (5) MR. BROWN: We'll have to hurry.

B. Ms. Smith reports the above conversation. Write her report of the conversation.
   (1) MS. SMITH: Mr. Brown said they were going to be late.
   (2) MS. SMITH: ....
   (3) MS. SMITH: ....
   (4) MS. SMITH: ....
   (5) MS. SMITH: ....

C. **Mr. Brown now reports the conversation he had with Mr. White. Write his report of the conversation.**

(1) MR. BROWN: I told Mr. White that ....
(2) MR. BROWN: ....
(3) MR. BROWN: ....
(4) MR. BROWN: ....
(5) MR. BROWN: ....

EXERCISE 34.1 | Indirect Speech: Adverbials of Time and Place
Complete the reported sentences, using an appropriate adverbial of time.
Example:

        [Wednesday]
        MISS BROWN: "I saw him yesterday."

        [Friday]
        REPORTER: She said she'd seen him the day before.
                      (or *on Tuesday,* or *the previous day.*)

1. [Monday, June 19]
   MR. PALMER: "I'm leaving for Japan tomorrow."
   [Thursday]
   REPORTER: Mr. Palmer said he was leaving for Japan ....

2. [Friday, May 10]
   [the Browns' house]
   MRS. BROWN: "My husband's not here now."
   [Monday, May 13]
   [the post office]
   REPORTER: She told me her husband wasn't ....

3. [7:00 p.m., Monday]
   MR. FAMA: "I'll call you tomorrow afternoon."
   [11:00 a.m., Tuesday]
   REPORTER: Mr. Fama said he'd call me ....

4. [Monday, August 1]
   TOM: "Come downtown with me day after tomorrow."

   [Tuesday, August 2]
   REPORTER: Tom asked me to go downtown with him ....

5. [Friday, March 6]
   MR. SIMPSON: "The work will be finished next week."

   [Tuesday, March 9]
   REPORTER: He told me the work would be finished ....

6. [Tuesday, January 15]
   [New York]
   MR. BLAKE: "I saw Bill here last week."

   [Tuesday, January 22]
   [New York]
   REPORTER: Mr. Blake told me he'd seen Bill ....

7. [February, 1970]
   MRS. PALMER: "I visited the Philippines two years ago."

   [March, 1972]
   REPORTER: Mrs. Palmer told me she visited the Philippines ....

8. [Wednesday, May 16]
   MR. BROWN: "I'll talk with Henry this morning."

   [Thursday, May 17]
   REPORTER: Mr. Brown said he'd talk with Henry ....

9. [11:30 a.m., Friday]
   MR. FERGUSON: "I saw Roger a few minutes ago."

   [3:00 p.m., Friday]
   REPORTER: He told me he saw Roger ....

10. [July, 1971]
    BARBARA: "I was sixteen last month."

    [September, 1971]
    REPORTER: Barbara told me she was sixteen ....

EXERCISE 34.2 | Summary Exercise: Practice in Reporting Speech

Read these statements. This is what Jim was saying to his friend Elmer.

1. "This is the first company dinner dance I've come to."
2. "The company holds all its parties here."
3. "I brought Jean with me."
4. "I've taken her out a few times."
5. "She's a very nice girl."
6. "I'm sure they'll serve a nice dinner."
7. "I know we'll have a good time."
8. "I'll have to take Jean home a little early tonight."
9. "I can't stay up late tonight."
10. "I have to catch a seven a.m. plane tomorrow morning."

Helen and Jean are roommates. It's noon the day after the dance and Helen is reporting to Jean everything she overheard. Complete the sentences. In some cases both words are correct.

1. He said .... *(this, that)* was the first company dance he .... *(had, would)* .... *(come, gone)* to.

2. Then he said the company .... *(holds, held)* all its parties .... *(here, there)*

3. He said he .... *(brought, took)* .... *(you, her)* with .... *(me, him)*

4. He said he had .... *(brought, taken)* .... *(you, her)* out a few times .... *(before, after)*.

5. He said you .... *(were, are)* a nice girl.

6. He said he .... *(is, was)* sure they .... *(would, will)* have a nice dinner.

7. He said he knew .... *(you, we)* .... *(will, would)* have a good time.

8. He said he .... *(would have to, must)* take .... *(her, you)* home a little early though.

9. He said he .... *(can't, couldn't)* stay up late .... *(tonight, last night)*.

10. He said he .... *(had to, has to)* catch a seven a.m. plane .... *(tomorrow morning, this morning)*.

SECTION 9

Verb + Infinitive
Special Verb Expressions
Adjective + Infinitive
Verb or Adjective + Infinitive: Short Answers
Infinitive of Purpose

---

35 Verb + Infinitive

- An infinitive (or **to** verb) consists of the word **to** and the base form of a verb (*to call, to know, to be,* etc.)

- A number of verbs in English can be followed by an infinitive. These are a few of them. (For a more complete list see the appendix, page 197.)

ask	decide	hope	promise
attempt	expect	need	want
choose	fail	plan	wish

Extra Drill 35.1

PRACTICE

Substitute.

Tom's planning	*to call* you tomorrow.
I want	....
He hopes	....
I'd like	....
He was expecting	....
I won't fail	....
She doesn't need	....
I promise	....
They'll try	....

- Sometimes two or more of these verbs + infinitive come in a row.

   Judd *wants to try to paint* the barn himself.

PRACTICE

Substitute progressively.

SUBJECT	VERB	INFINITIVE
John	wants	to go.

TEACHER	STUDENT
Bob	Bob wants to go.
plan	....
to call	....
Past Tense	
expect	....
decide	....
Helen	....
want	....
Yes/No Question	
promise	....
to help	....
need	Did Helen need to help?

EXERCISE 35.1 | Verb + Infinitive. See page 129.

Extra Drill 35.2-4

36 Special Verb Expressions

- There is a small group of verb expressions that are somewhat different from ordinary verbs. They express meanings similar to some of the modals.

- Those in which the verb *BE* is a part of the idiom are *be to, be able to, be going to, be about to* and *be supposed to*. Two others which do not use *BE* are *have to* and *used to*. These expressions are always followed by the base form of a verb.

- **Be to + verb.** Only the present and past tenses of the verb *BE (am, is, are, was, were)* are used with this structure. It expresses an action that is scheduled or arranged to take place.

  Mrs. Jones told her students to arrive at exactly 8:00.
  She said, "You *are to be* here at exactly 8:00."

  She told them where their examination would take place.
  She said, "The exam *is to be* in room 237."

  Mr. Brown came at 3:00 for a meeting.
  Mr. Wells said to him, "Didn't you know the meeting *was to begin* at 2:30?"

Extra Drill 36.1

- **Be able to + verb.** This expression means the same as the modal *can*. It is used to express ability. *Be able to* is used in many sentences when it is not possible to use the modal *can* (in perfect verb phrases, for example).

    I hope *to be able to come.*
    When *will* you *be able to tell* me?
    I *haven't been able to see* him.
    Were you *able to translate* the sentences?

- **Be about to + verb.** This idiom is used to tell of an action that is going to happen almost immediately.

    Mr. Brown is putting on his coat. He*'s about to leave.*
    I had my hand on the door. I *was about to close* it when the phone rang.

> ### PRACTICE
>
> **Answer "No" and then add a sentence in the present tense using *"be about to."* Use pronouns.**
>
> | SPEAKER A | SPEAKER B |
> |---|---|
> | 1. Has John gone yet? | No, but he's about to go. |
> | 2. Has the meeting begun? | .... |
> | 3. Has the plane landed yet? | .... |
> | 4. Did they buy the house? | .... |
> | 5. Have you finished the book yet? | .... |

When used in the negative, the meaning of *be about to* is usually quite different. If a speaker says, "I'm not about to go," he means that he *will not go*. He is determined *not* to go. The word *about* is often spoken louder than the other words in the sentence. Here are a few examples:

I won't tell John.	I'm *not abóut to tell* him anything.
She wouldn't sell her ring.	She *wasn't abóut to sell* it.

> ### PRACTICE
>
> **Answer in the present tense using** *"not about to."* **Use pronouns.**
>
> | | TEACHER | STUDENT |
> |---|---|---|
> | 1. | Will you tell John? | No, and I'm not about to tell him. |
> | 2. | Did Helen sell her watch? | No, and .... |
> | 3. | Have you seen the new movie? | No, and .... |
> | 4. | Has Mary called Bill? | No, and .... |
> | 5. | Did June invite Barbara? | No, and .... |

- **Be going to + verb.** One of the ways of expressing future time in English is by using a form of *be going to.*

    We're *going to go* on a picnic tomorrow.

    In the past tense, *be going to* often tells about something that was planned or intended to happen, but which did not actually take place.

    We *were going to go* on a picnic, but it rained.

- **Be supposed to + verb.** This verb expression is similar in meaning to *ought to.*

    Aunt Ann *is supposed to arrive* tomorrow morning.
    John *was supposed to call* me, but he didn't.
    You're *not supposed to do* that.

    > **Extra Drill 36.2**

    It may also tell of an action that is planned or is expected to take place in the future.

    I think it's *supposed to rain* this afternoon.

- **Have to + verb.** The meaning of *have to* and *must* is practically the same.

    Since *must* has no past tense, a form of *have to* is used when it is necessary to describe a strong obligation in the past.

    We *must study* harder.   We *had to study* late last night.

- **Used to + verb.** This expression (pronounced /yuwstə/ is used only in the past tense. It tells of an action that formerly took place, but which does not take place now.

    I *used to live* there, but I don't anymore.
    We *used to swim* in the ocean everyday.

    The auxiliary *did* is used in questions and negatives.

    Craig *didn't use to drive* a yellow sports car.

PRACTICE

Practice the dialog.

JIM: We*'re about to go* swimming. *Aren't* you *going to come* with us?
TED: No, I *won't be able to* today.
JIM: Why not?
TED: Dad told me *I had to do* some work. He says I*'m supposed to work* around the house an hour a day.
JIM: What*'re* you *supposed to do?*
TED: Whatever needs to be done.
JIM: You*'re going to come* to the meeting, aren't you?
TED: Oh, sure. I*'m not about to miss* that. When is it?
JIM: Tonight at 8:30 sharp. It*'s to be* at Henry's house this time.

EXERCISE 36.1 | Yes/No Questions and Short Answers. See page 129.

Extra Drill 36.3-4

37 Adjective + Infinitive

- There are a number of adjectives that can be followed by infinitives.

   I'm *sorry to hear* that.   He seemed *afraid to tell* us.

These are a few of the adjectives that can be followed by infinitives. (For a more complete list see the appendix, page 197.)

afraid	delighted	pleased	sorry
anxious	glad	proud	sure
careful	happy	ready	willing

EXERCISE 37.1 | Verb or Adjective + Infinitive. See page 130.
EXERCISE 37.2 | Verb or Adjective + Infinitive. See page 130.

Extra Drill 37.1

38 Verb or Adjective + Infinitive: Short Answers

- To answer a question using any of the verbs or adjectives above, either the appropriate auxiliary, or the verb or adjective + *to* can be used.

   Is she going to call us?   Are we supposed to come?
     Yes, she is.   Yes, we are.
     She*'s going to.*   We*'re supposed to.*

   Does he want to go?   Are you anxious to go?
     No, he doesn't.   Yes, I am.
     He *doesn't want to.*   I*'m anxious to.*

SECTION NINE

In conversation it is very common to omit the base verb following a *verb* + *to* or an *adjective* + *to* expression. It is understood what verb should follow *to*.

> Are you going to the lecture?
> I'm not sure *I want to*. (go)
>
> Why are you helping Jack?
> Because *I promised to*. (help him)
>
> Are you going to work today?
> *I'm not anxious to* (go), but I suppose *I'll have to*. (go)
>
> I don't want to go, but *I have to*. (go)
>
> He didn't do it because *he was afraid to*. (do it)

EXERCISE 38.1 | Verb or Adjective + Infinitive: Short Answers. See page 130.

Extra Drill 38.1-3

39 Infinitive of Purpose

- Many infinitives that follow verbs express purpose. An infinitive used in this way is called an *infinitive of purpose*.

  > John stopped *to talk* to Mr. Wilson.

- The infinitive in this sentence tells *why* John stopped. It gives the reason or purpose for which John stopped. The reason John stopped was *in order to* talk to Mr. Wilson. If an infinitive of purpose is being used it is always possible to use *in order to* in place of *to*. The use of *in order to* emphasizes the expression of purpose.

  > Mary called *to thank* us.
  > Mary called *in order to thank* us.

- How can we tell whether an infinitive is being used to express purpose? The infinitive of purpose answers a question using *why?* From the sentence *John stopped to talk to Mr. Wilson,* we can form the question "Why did John stop?" The answer is "To talk," or "In order to talk." "To talk" then, is an infinitive of purpose in this sentence.

PRACTICE

Use infinitive of purpose. Use pronouns when needed.

1. Jean called Bob and said, "I want to tell you the good news."
   Why did Jean call Bob? To tell him the good news.

2. Helen went to her mother and said, "I want to help you."
   Why did Helen go to her mother? . . . .

3. Mr. Brown said to his wife, "I went downtown to buy a new pair of shoes for myself."
   Why did Mr. Brown go downtown? . . . .

4. Mrs. Wells stopped by Mrs. Chase's house and said, "I want to give you some flowers."
   Why did Mrs. Wells stop by Mrs. Chase's house? . . . .

5. Ted went to George's house and said, "I'd like to see your new bike."
   Why did Ted go to George's house? . . . .

EXERCISE 39.1 | Infinitive of Purpose. See page 131.
EXERCISE 39.2 | Infinitive of Purpose. See page 131.

Extra Drill 39.1

SECTION 10

Verb + Gerund
Preposition + Gerund
Verbs Followed by Either Gerunds or Infinitives
Gerunds and Infinitives as Subjects and Complements
"It" and "There" as Sentence Subjects

40 Verb + Gerund

> **Study these sentences.**
> 1. He admitted *taking* the money.
> 2. I suggested *leaving* early.
> 3. Do you believe in *doing* your best?
> 4. We're looking forward to *seeing* you.
> 5. Don't be afraid of *making* mistakes.
> 6. We weren't very excited about *going*.

- A *gerund* is the **-ing** form of a verb used as a noun phrase (NP).
- A gerund may be used as the object of a transitive verb. These are some of the verbs in English that can be followed by a gerund. (For a more complete list see the appendix, page 198.)

admit	enjoy	recommend
advise	finish	resent
consider	include	risk
deny	postpone	suggest

- Because gerunds are verb forms, they can have objects or complements, and they can be followed by adverbs or adverbial phrases.

> He likes *teaching English*. (gerund + object)
> I recommend *leaving early*. (gerund + adverb)

| Extra Drill 40.1 |

41 Preposition + Gerund

- A gerund may be used as the object of a preposition.

- Some verbs are followed regularly by certain prepositions. Many of these can be followed by gerunds.

    I *thought of taking* a trip.
    We *talked about giving* a party.

    These are some of the verbs that are often used with certain prepositions, and which can be followed by gerunds. (For a more complete list see the appendix, page 200.)

ask about	forget about	talk about
believe in	laugh about	tell about
depend on	look forward to	tell of
end with	pay for	worry about
fight about	speak of	

- Some two-word verbs can also be followed by gerunds.

    | give up | go on | keep on | put off |

PRACTICE

Substitute progressively.

He considered buying a new house.

want	He wanted to buy a new house.
give up	....
car	....
I	....
hope	....
put off	....
they	....
decide	They decided to buy a new car.

- A number of adjectives in English are commonly used with certain prepositions. Gerunds can follow these prepositions, too. These are a few of them. (For a more complete list see the appendix, page 200.)

afraid of	particular about
careful about	proud of
excited about	sad about
famous for	tired of (from)
good at	successful in

> # PRACTICE
>
> **Speaker B replies in terms of the statement of fact, using a gerund in the reply.**
>
> STATEMENT OF FACT
> 1. Mary said, "I didn't break the dish."
> 2. Johnny said, "I don't want to fly. I'm afraid."
> 3. Helen said, "I like to play tennis."
> 4. Mr. Brown said, "I think I'll buy a new car."
> 5. Mr. Sanborn said, "I think we should pay attention to what John says."
>
> | SPEAKER A | SPEAKER B |
> |---|---|
> | 1. What did Mary deny doing? | *She denied breaking the dish.* |
> | 2. What's Johnny afraid of doing? | .... |
> | 3. What does Helen enjoy? | .... |
> | 4. What is Mr. Brown thinking of doing? | .... |
> | 5. What does Mr. Sanborn suggest? | .... |

Extra Drill 41.1-2

EXERCISE 41.1 | Practice with Gerunds After Verbs and Prepositions. See page 132.

- To give short answers to questions using a verb or preposition + gerund, the appropriate auxiliary may be used.

    Do you enjoy working?   Yes, I do.
    Are they interested in going? Yes, they are.

Extra Drill 41.3

- When a main verb or adjective is used in the answer, the gerund is usually replaced by the pronoun **it**.

    Did he consider *going*?   Yes, he considered *it*.
    Do you think he's worried about *flying*?   Yes, he's quite worried about *it*.

Extra Drill 41.4

After an intransitive verb *it* is not needed as a gerund substitute.

    Have you finished *working*?   Yes, I've finished.
    Did you forget *about going*?   Yes, I forgot.

- If the gerund has an object or modifiers, both the gerund and the associated words can be replaced by *that* or by the phrase *doing that*.

>Do you enjoy *telling stories?*   Yes, I enjoy *that.*
>Would you prefer *riding with us?*   Yes, I'd much prefer *doing that.*

PRACTICE

A. Use *it* in the answer to substitute for the gerund and any following words.

1. Did he admit *losing the book?*   Yes, he did. He admitted *it.*
2. Did she deny *taking the money?*   Yes, ...
3. Will they resent *having to use their car?*   No, ...
4. Have they recommended *building a new library?*   No, ...

B. Use *doing that* to substitute for the gerund and any following words.

1. Do you suggest *leaving early in the morning?*   Yes, I do. I suggest *doing that.*
2. Has he considered *borrowing the money he needs?*   Yes, ...
3. Are they looking forward to *taking a camping trip?*   Yes, ...
4. Will your work include *making plans for new school buildings?*   No, ...

---

42 Verbs Followed by Either Infinitives or Gerunds

- There are some verbs which can be followed by either a gerund or an infinitive with little or no difference in meaning.

>It *began to rain.*
>It *began raining.*

Some common verbs of this type are these. (For a more complete list see the appendix, page 198.)

attempt	hate	like	prefer
begin	hesitate	love	start
continue	intend	neglect	remember
dread	learn	plan	try

EXERCISE 42.1 | Using Infinitives and Gerunds. See page 133.

EXERCISE 42.2 | Summary Exercise: Using Infinitives and Gerunds. See page 133.

EXERCISE 42.3 | Summary Exercise: Using Infinitives and Gerunds. See page 134.

43 Gerunds and Infinitives as Subjects and Complements

- Gerunds and infinitives are often called *verbal nouns*. As noun phrases (NPs), they may be used as subjects or complements.

   Learning is important.   *To learn* is important.
   Seeing is *believing*.   Your job is *to cook the food*.

   > Extra Drill 43.1

- Both infinitives and gerunds are verb forms and they have verb qualities. For example, they are made negative by the use of the word *not*.

   Not to go would be rude.
   Not to decide is to decide.

   Not knowing was very difficult for them.
   Not studying was his mistake.

   > Extra Drill 43.2

Both may have objects and complements, and they may be followed by adverbs or adverbial phrases.

   Preparing the food is her job.   *Walking fast* is good exercise.
   To see him was a surprise.   *Swimming every day* is healthy.
   Being president was his hope.   *To decide immediately* was
   To be lost is no fun.   necessary.

EXERCISE 43.1 | Forming Gerund Phrases. See page 135.

44 *It* and *There* as Sentence Subjects

- The word **it** is frequently used in subject position. A singular form of *BE* or a linking verb follows *it*.

   It was a pleasure to meet you.
   It is nice seeing you.
   It became boring after an hour.

- A sentence which has an infinitive as subject can be changed to a sentence using **it** in subject position. Sentences beginning with **it** are the more usual usage.

   To learn is difficult.   To visit New Mexico is a great idea.
   It's difficult to learn.   *It's a great idea to visit New Mexico.*

> ## PRACTICE
>
> **Change the sentence to one using *it* in subject position. Then form a question by preceding your transformed sentence with "Do you think..."**
>
> 1. To study is important.
>   *Do you think it's important to study?*
> 2. To swim in the ocean seems easy.
>   ....
> 3. To be able to speak a foreign language is useful.
>   ....
> 4. To build a fire will be difficult.
>   ....
> 5. To picnic by the river would be pleasant.
>   ....

Extra Drill 44.1-2

- The word **there** is very commonly used in subject position. It has no real meaning and is often called an "empty" subject. The true subject follows the verb and determines whether the verb is singular or plural. *There* is used before *BE* and a few other verbs *(appear, come, go, happen, remain, seem)*.

>   There's some food in the kitchen.
>   Were there many schools there?
>   There won't be time in the afternoon.
>   There seem to be only a few people there.
>   There remained two more problems to solve.

- A sentence with an indefinite noun phrase as the subject of the verb *BE* can be changed to a sentence beginning with *there*.

>   *Some fish are* in the river.
>   *There are some fish* in the river.
>
>   *A bird's* on the roof.
>   *There's a bird* on the roof.

SECTION TEN

> **PRACTICE**
>
> **Change the sentences so that *there* is used in subject position.**
>
> 1. A large table was in the dining room.
>   *There was a large table in the dining room.*
> 2. A silk purse was in her hand.
>   ....
> 3. A few birds were in the trees.
>   ....
> 4. A young boy was at the door.
>   ....
> 5. Several coins were in his pocket.
>   ....

Extra Drill 44.3

- Sentences with continuous verb forms may also be changed to sentences with *there* in a subject position.

     Some men are working here.
  There are some men   working here.

     Only a few people were listening.
  There were only a few people   listening.

Extra Drill 44.4

EXERCISE 44.1 | Using *there* in Subject Position. See page 135.

- The "empty" subject *there* is not the same as the place adverb *there*. "Empty" subject *there* usually has weak stress; place adverbs *there* and *here* have stronger stress.

  ("empty" subject)   *Thĕre's some cóffee for you on that table.*

  ("empty" subject)   *Thĕre's some cóffee for you—over thére.*
  (place adverb)

  (place adverb)   *Thére's your coffee—over thére.* (place adverb)

  (place adverb)   *Hĕre's some cóffee for you.*

118 GRAMMAR AND DRILLBOOK

SECTION 11

*Nominal Phrases
Noun Compounds*

45 Nominal Phrases

- A **nominal phrase** consists of two nouns. The first noun modifies the second, and often tells what kind of material the second noun is made of.

    brick house   wool suit   straw hat

- In a nominal phrase, the second noun usually receives stronger stress than the first.

    grâss skírt   sîlver wátch
    stône hóuse   plâstic spóons

PRACTICE

Repeat the noun phrases and sentences.

wôol cóat	She's wearing a wôol cóat.
gold ring	He gave her a gold ring.
brick house	We're building a brick house.
côtton dréss	She bought a côtton dréss.
paper plates	We need some paper plates.
silver watch	I own a silver watch.

Extra Drill 45.1-4

- A premodifying noun follows all adjectives and comes immediately before the noun it modifies.

DETERMINER	DESCRIPTIVE ADJECTIVE	SIZE AND AGE	COLOR	ORIGIN	PREMODIFYING NOUN	MODIFIED NOUN
a	beautiful	new	blue	French	silk	dress
some	nice	new	brown		leather	shoes
a	long		yellow		summer	coat

Extra Drill 45.5

- When two or more nominal phrases with the same modified noun occur, it is possible to use the substitute word *one* (or *ones*) in place of the second noun.

    He bought a gold *ring* and a silver *ring*.
    He bought a gold *ring* and a silver *one*.

    Mary wears wool *dresses;* the other girls wear cotton *ones*.

PRACTICE

Use the cue word followed by *one* or *ones*. Stress the modifier in your sentences.

TEACHER	STUDENT
1. I live in a stone house. *brick*	Mrs. Brown *lives in a brick one.*
2. Helen's wearing a wool suit. *cotton*	Mary ....
3. I have a silver watch. *gold*	He ....
4. Those aren't steel spoons. *plastic*	They're ....
5. I use cloth napkins. *paper*	She ....

Extra Drill 45.6-7

- Time words, place words and many others can also be used as premodifying nouns.

    summer day   city street   family argument
    winter weather   state police   noun compound

EXERCISE 45.1 | Word Order of Noun Modifiers. See page 136.

46 Noun Compounds

- A *noun compound* is made up of two words, but it is a unit. The two words together are like a single noun in English. The first word is spoken with stronger stress than the second.

Observe the examples. Repeat the words and sentences.

textbook	barber shop	record player
campground	coffee cup	apple orchard
raincoat	tennis shoes	station wagon
airport	dinner plate	flower garden

1. Have you seen my textbook?
2. Where's the campground?
3. They bought a station wagon.
4. I can't find my tennis shoes.

Extra Drill 46.1

PRACTICE

Begin the answers with "It's called" or "They're called," as appropriate.

	SPEAKER A	SPEAKER B
1.	What's *a platter for meat* called?	It's called a meat platter.
2.	What are *books about grammar* called?	....
3.	What's *a bowl for sugar* called?	....
4.	What are *spoons for soup* called?	....
5.	What's *cream for coffee* called?	....
6.	What are *keys to the house* called?	....

- Often both parts of a noun compound are nouns, with the first noun sometimes in possessive form. Not all noun compounds are combinations of two nouns, however. Observe the following examples.

  doctor's office (possessive + noun)   repairman (verb + noun)

  fishing village (gerund + noun)   drive-in (verb + adverb)

  blueprint (adjective + noun)   back rub (noun + verb)

Extra Drill 46.2-3

PRACTICE

Begin the answers with "It's called" or "They're called."

	TEACHER	STUDENT
1.	What's *water for drinking* called?	It's called drinking water.
2.	What are *materials for building* called?	....
3.	What's an *office for a lawyer* called?	....
4.	What's a *pool for swimming* called?	....

SECTION ELEVEN

- The plural of a noun compound is formed by adding the plural ending to the second word. The first word is generally used in singular form, although there are exceptions such as *salesman*. If the second word is a mass noun (*water, milk,* etc.), then appropriate noun determiners or containers are used with the noun compound.

    two shoe stores   a glass of drinking water
    a few postage stamps   a little spending money
    several water glasses   not much goat's milk

PRACTICE
Begin the answers with "It's called" or "They're called."

	SPEAKER A	SPEAKER B
1.	What's *a store that sells groceries* called?	It's called a grócery stòre.
2.	What are *shops that sell dresses* called?	....
3.	What's *a factory that makes toys* called?	....
4.	What are *stores that sell candy* called?	....

- With a noun compound, it is not possible to use the substitute *one* or *ones* to replace the second word.

    Does she have a flower garden or a vegetable garden?
    She has a flower garden.

    Because "flower garden" is a noun compound, we cannot say *a flower one*. We must say the whole compound *flower garden*.

- How can you recognize a noun compound? In writing, if the two words are written as one word, then you can be sure that it is a noun compound. However, many compounds (and all nominal phrases) are written as two words.

    The only way to be sure of a noun compound is to listen to the stress when it is said by itself (that is, in isolation). If the first word is spoken louder than the second, it is a *noun compound*. If the last word has the stronger stress, it is a *nominal phrase*.

Extra Drill 46.4-6

PRACTICE
NOUN COMPOUNDS AND NOMINAL PHRASES

Listen to the following. If the strong stress is on the first word, put an "X" under "Noun compound." If the strong stress is on the second word, put an "X" under "Nominal phrase."*

TEACHER	NOUN COMPOUND	NOMINAL PHRASE
1. schoolboy	X	
2. steel knife		X
3. butter knife		
4. rubber ball		
5. postage stamp		
6. summer rain		
7. asking price		
8. wool sweater		
9. silk umbrella		
10. sweet potato		
11. toy store		
12. toy gun		

- Strong stress used for contrast overrides the usual rules for noun phrases and noun compounds.

NORMAL STRESS	CONTRAST STRESS
Let me see those rubber gloves.	They're leather gloves, sir.
I saw you get in a police wagon.	It was a police car, sir.

EXERCISE 46.1 | Noun Compounds. See page 137.
EXERCISE 46.2 | Noun Compounds. See page 138.

*Note to the teacher: The noun compounds are numbers 1, 3, 5, 7, 10, and 11.

SECTION 12

Compound Noun Phrases
Conjunctions with Other Structures
The Conjunction "but"
Special Nouns in Reference to Number

47 Compound Noun Phrases

> **Study these sentences.**
> 1. I drink both tea and coffee.
> 2. Both Jean and Ruth are my good friends.
> 3. I don't have a pen or pencil.
> 4. He had neither time nor money.
> 5. I can give you either an apple or an orange.
> 6. Neither Bob nor Lisa could help me.
> 7. Either your father or mother should come.

- The words **and** and **or** are conjunctions. They join sentences or parts of sentences. They often join two noun phrases.

    Tom and John   Tom or John
    the boys and girls   the boys or girls

- Two noun phrases (NPs) joined by *and* or *or* form a *compound noun phrase*.

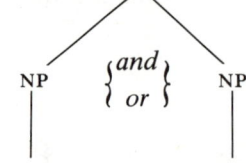

    History   and geography are my best subjects.
    Martha   or Barbara will help you.

- When used as subject, two noun phrases joined by **and** take a plural verb.

    John and his brother *are* coming.
    His hat and coat *were* on the table

124 GRAMMAR AND DRILLBOOK

- When the same modifier could be used twice (*my* mother and *my* father), the second occurrence is generally omitted.

    my mother and *my* father ⟹ *my* mother and father
    some bread and *some* milk ⟹ *some* bread and milk.

    | Extra Drill 47.1-2 |

- Two singular noun phrases joined by **or** take a singular verb.

    My father or mother *is* usually home by six o'clock.

    If the second noun phrase is plural, then the verb will generally be plural.

    Mr. Smith or his sons *are* there.

    | Extra Drill 47.3-5 |

- A series of three or more noun phrases may be included in a compound noun phrase. In this case, the words *and* and *or* are generally used only between the last two noun phrases.

    In writing, a comma (,) is used between the phrases not connected by *and* or *or*.

    Mary, Jane and Helen are here.
    I bought a pen, two pencils, an eraser and a notebook.

EXERCISE 47.1 | Punctuation of Words in a Series. See page 139.

| Extra Drill 47.6 |

- The pairs of words **both...and, either...or,** and **neither...nor** are called *paired conjunctions*. Another term for them is *correlatives*.

- The paired conjunction *both...and* acts just as the conjunction *and* does.

    Both the pen *and* pencil are mine.

    | Extra Drill 47.7 |

- *Either...or* and *neither...nor* act just as the conjunction *or* does.

    Either Dr. Smith *or* his son was going to call us.
    Either my parents or his plan to drive.

    Neither Tom *nor* his brother goes to that school.
    Neither the teachers nor the students like grammar.

- *Neither...nor* cannot be used if there is another negative word in the sentence.

    I don't want either coffee or tea.
    I want neither coffee nor tea.

PRACTICE

TEACHER	STUDENT

A. Use *both...and.*
   1. Mary is coming.　　　　　　　　*Both Mary and Bill are*
      Bill is coming, too.　　　　　　　*coming.*

   2. I saw Helen.
      I saw her sister, too.　　　　　　................

   3. He told his father.
      He told his mother, too.　　　　　................

   4. Mr. Brown's an engineer.
      Mr. White's an engineer, too.　　　................

B. Use *neither...nor.*
   1. Mary wouldn't tell me.　　　　　*Neither Mary nor Helen*
      Helen wouldn't tell me either.　　*would tell me.*

   2. I didn't see June.
      I didn't see her brother either.　　................

   3. He wouldn't tell his father.
      He wouldn't tell his mother, either.　................

   4. He had no time.
      He had no money, either.　　　　................

EXERCISE 47.2| Using *neither...nor.* See page 139.

48 Conjunctions with Other Structures

- Conjunctions join structures that are similar. Thus, two adjectives may be connected.

    hard or easy　　　　　　　both big and tall
    warm and comfortable　　　neither tall nor short

- Conjunctions also join verb phrases.

    He neither *laughed* nor *smiled.*
    She *went downtown* and *bought a new coat.*

- When the same words are joined by a conjunction in a sentence, the second occurrence is usually omitted.

    You can stand up or *you can* sit down.
  ⇒ *You can* stand up or sit down.

    They were singing and *they were* laughing.
  ⇒ *They were* singing and laughing.

  EXERCISE 48.1 | Restating Sentences with Conjunctions. See page 139.

  > Extra Drill 48.1

49 The Conjunction *but*

> **Study these sentences.**
> 1. I didn't tell Mary, but I told Jean.
> 2. He studied, but he didn't pass the test.
> 3. I drink coffee but not tea.
> 4. I know John but not Tom.
> 5. He was poor but happy.
> 6. The taste was strange but good.
> 7. He was angry but not violent.
> 8. He was big but not strong.

- **But** is another conjunction which joins similar structures. The things that are connected by *but* may both be true, but they are generally opposite in meaning in some way.

  CONNECTING TWO SENTENCES

  I like coffee, but *I don't like tea.*
  I know John, but *I don't know Mary.*

  CONNECTING TWO NOUN PHRASES

  I like *coffee* but *not tea.*
  I know *John* but *not Mary.*

  CONNECTING TWO ADJECTIVES

  He was poor, but *he was happy.*
  The radio was cheap, but *it was good.*
  I like my steak rare, but *I don't like it raw.*
  The problem was hard, but *it wasn't impossible.*

  He was *poor* but *happy.*
  The radio was *cheap* but *good.*
  I like my steak *rare* but not *raw.*
  The problem was *hard* but not *impossible.*

  EXERCISE 49.1 | Practice with Conjunctions. See page 140.
  EXERCISE 49.2 | Sentence Completion: Practice with Conjunctions. See page 140.

  > Extra Drill 49.1-3

50 Special Nouns in Reference to Number

- There are a few nouns which are special in some way. The nouns *news* and *mathematics,* for example, end in "s" but always take a singular verb. The word *people,* on the other hand, takes a plural verb.

    The *news was* quite bad.
    People were beginning to come.

- Nouns which name a group of people, animals or things are called *collective nouns.* These nouns usually take a singular verb. (It is possible to use a plural verb with them if the members of the group are thought of separately.) The words *family* and *crowd* are examples of collective nouns.

    My *family is* coming with me.
    The *crowd was* angry.

- The names of a few countries are plural in form, but they take a singular verb.

    The United States is a large country.
    The Netherlands is in Europe.

- Some common pairs of words are always said in a certain order when they are thought of as a unit. *Bread and butter,* for example, is always said in this way, never *butter and bread.* The following pairs also have a fixed word order.

    knife and fork   ham and eggs
    husband and wife   shoes and socks
    salt and pepper   cup and saucer

- Considered as one unit, these take a singular verb.

    The bread and butter's on the table.
    Where's the salt and pepper?
    This cup and saucer is dirty.

    But when not used as a unit:

    Bread and butter are important staples.

- When used as the subject of a verb, the expression *the number* takes a singular verb. If we say *a number,* however, the plural verb is used.

    The number of houses *was* small.
    (*number* is subject)

    A number of men *were* waiting.
    (*men* is subject; *number of* is a predeterminer.)

EXERCISE 50.1 | Subject and Verb Agreement. See page 140.

| Extra Drill 50.1 |

EXERCISES FOR SECTIONS 9-12

Exercises for Section 9

EXERCISE 35.1 | Verb + Infinitive

Take the part of Speaker B and answer the question. Use the cued words.

EXAMPLE: SPEAKER A: Did you promise to bring custard? *(bring potato salad)*
 SPEAKER B: Yes, but I didn't promise to bring potato salad.

1. Did you promise to pick up Judy? *(take her home)*
2. Did you attempt to reduce the electric bill? *(reduce the gas bill)*
3. Did she try to tune the piano? *(play it)*
4. Does she want to speak to Mr. Adams? *(interrupt him)*
5. Does he expect to make it to Cleveland today? *(meet Mr. Collier today)*
6. Does he need to wear a hat? *(take an umbrella)*
7. Do they want to eat Chinese food? *(use chopsticks)*
8. Do you wish to have dessert? *(order it now)*

EXERCISE 36.1 | Yes/No Questions and Short Answers

A. Speaker A forms a Yes/No question from each statement of fact. Speaker B gives a short answer based on the statement of fact. Note: From all negative statements, be sure to form a simple Yes/No question, not a negative question. See the example for #2 below.

STATEMENT OF FACT	SPEAKER A	SPEAKER B
1. He's supposed to come tomorrow.	1. Is he supposed to come tomorrow?	Yes, he is.
2. It wasn't supposed to rain.	2. Was it supposed to rain?	No, it wasn't. |//
3. They've decided to go.		
4. She won't be able to help us.		
5. He has to get a haircut.		
6. He isn't willing to drive.		
7. She was pleased to hear the news.		
8. Mrs. White expects to be home this afternoon.		
9. John hasn't been able to save any money.		
10. They're going to take tennis lessons.		
11. We'll need to tell them when we're going.		

B. **Speaker A uses the statement of fact and forms a tag question. Speaker B gives the expected short answer.**

1. He's supposed to come tomorrow, isn't he?   Yes, he is.
2. It wasn't supposed to rain, was it?   No, it wasn't

Continue.

EXERCISE 37.1 | Verb or Adjective + Infinitive
Give complete sentences in answer to the questions, using a verb or adjective + infinitive.

1. What do you like to do in the evening?
2. What are you hoping to do in the next few years?
3. Are there things in life you have to do?
4. Are you afraid to do anything?
5. What is the most important thing you've ever learned to do?
6. What is the hardest thing you've ever attempted to do?
7. Is there anything that you are very anxious to do?
8. Why do you want to learn to speak English?

EXERCISE 37.2 | Verb or Adjective + Infinitive
Write a short paragraph. Tell what you are planning or hoping to do in the next year or two. Use several verbs and adjectives such as *hope, want, expect, anxious*, which are followed by infinitives.

You might start like this:
Next year I want to ....

EXERCISE 38.1 | Verb or Adjective + Infinitive: Short Answers
Give short Yes/No answers to the questions. Use *to* in the answer *if it is possible to do so*. If it is not possible, use the auxiliary (See example below).

Example:	Are you going to see him?	Yes, *I'm going to.*
	Was he afraid to stay alone?	No, *he wasn't afraid to.*
	Did he worry about going?	Yes, *he did.*

1. Are they about to leave him?   Yes, ...
2. Was she able to tell him?   No, ...
3. Are we supposed to call first?   Yes, ...
4. Are you going to pack the car now?   Yes, ...
5. Are they anxious to go?   No, ...
6. Does he enjoy camping?   Yes, ...
7. Have they finished working?   No, ...

8. Did she want to memorize the dialog?   No, ...
9. Are they sad about leaving?   Yes, ...
10. Do they intend to go?   Yes, ...

EXERCISE 39.1 | Infinitive of Purpose

If the sentence contains an infinitive of purpose, replace *to* with *in order to*.

Examples: He called to invite me to lunch.
He called in order to invite me to lunch.
She plans to invite us to lunch soon.
(No change possible: not an infinitive of purpose.)

1. He studied hard to pass the examination.
2. I hope to see you soon.
3. He called to tell me about his new car.
4. We had to run to catch the bus.
5. They promised to call us soon.
6. I took the plane to save time.
7. Mr. Jones told his son to get a haircut.
8. John sold his bicycle to get some money.
9. He's going to night school to finish his education.
10. Dr. White walks a mile every day to get some exercise.

EXERCISE 39.2 | Infinitive of Purpose

Change the sentences. Replace the *for*-phrase with an infinitive of purpose.

1. I stopped at school *for my daughter*.
   I stopped to get my daughter at school (*or*) to pick up my daughter.
2. We stopped for lunch.
3. We went out for a walk.
4. I wrote to the company for some information.
5. I looked in the dictionary for the meaning of the word.
6. There's a new Chinese restaurant where we should go for dinner.
7. I went to the post office for some stamps.
8. I need some medicine for my cold.
9. She reached across the table for the butter.
10. I stayed in the hotel room for some much needed rest.

Exercises for Section 10

EXERCISE 41.1 | Practice with Gerunds after Verbs and Prepositions

Answer the questions in accordance with the pictures. In all cases use a gerund form in your reply. Replace names with pronouns.

1.

What did Mary suggest?

2.

What are Mr. and Mrs. Palmer looking forward to?

3.

What is Mr. Star about to finish?

4.

What is John good at?

5.

What is Jane trying to give up?

6.

What is Laura excited about?

7.

What do the grandchildren enjoy?

8.

What did Mrs. Falk admit doing?

EXERCISE 42.1 | Using Infinitives and Gerunds

Read the sentences, changing the infinitive to a gerund or the gerund to an infinitive *if it is possible to do so*. Do not change any other words in the sentence.

Examples: Do you prefer *driving?*
Do you prefer *to drive?*

Do you enjoy *camping?*
(No change possible.)

1. We forgot about *going*.
2. I resented *hearing* about it.
3. I didn't want *to tell* him about it.
4. She intends *to tell* him.
5. He sat down and began *to read* a book.
6. We decided *to leave* suddenly.
7. He started *learning* Spanish when he was ten.
8. They're tired from *working* so hard all day.
9. I'm very sorry *to hear* that.
10. He hates *to spend* money.
11. You were very clever *to find out*.
12. Everyone dreaded *to go*.
13. All six employees threatened *to quit*.
14. We debated *leaving* but decided against it.
15. We felt we were unqualified *to judge* the matter.
16. Do you ever avoid *saying* hello to people you don't like?

EXERCISE 42.2 | Summary Exercise: Using Infinitives and Gerunds

Read the sentences using an infinitive, gerund or base form of the verb in parentheses. In some sentences more than one form is correct.

(go)	1. Why do you want ....?	*Why do you want to go?*
(swim)	2. She doesn't like	*She doesn't like to swim./She doesn't like swimming.*
(fly)	3. He's not afraid of .... but he doesn't like it.	
(tell)	4. Why do you think he was afraid .... us?	
(do)	5. What do you expect me ....?	
(return)	6. Did he promise .... the money?	
(thank)	7. She called .... me for the tickets.	
(take)	8. They're looking forward to .... a trip.	
(write)	9. Please continue	

(go)   10. I can't .... now. I'll have to put off .... until next year.
(wash)   11. Have you finished .... the car?
(fix)   12. Have you paid him for .... the stove?
(do)   13. Do you know what he intends .... about it?
(take)   14. I prefer .... train.
(do)   15. Many women don't like .... housework.
(rain)   16. It began .... about 2:00.
(cook)   17. His job at camp is .... the food.
(teach)   18. Mrs. Jones said she's tired of ....
(lose)   19. Why did he risk .... all his money?
(thank)   20. I telephoned .... them for the invitation.
(be)   21. If I go now, he's sure .... in his office.
(do)   22. He's always very careful .... the right thing.
(memorize) 23. She's very good at ....
(buy)   24. He asked me, "Have you ever considered .... an apartment?"
(go)   25. Why shouldn't we .... if we want to?
(have)   26. He asked me, "Would you prefer .... the meeting at 2:00 or 3:00?
(tell)   27. He said he intended .... us all about it.
(read)   28. Did you enjoy .... the book?
(work)   29. They said, "We're tired of .... seven days a week."
(do)   30. It's my turn to finish .... the exercise.

EXERCISE 42.3 | Summary Exercise: Using Infinitives and Gerunds

Using the pairs of words below, form questions to ask other members of the class.

Examples: like/go   *Would you like to go to the movies tonight?*
              good at/play   *Are you very good at playing tennis?*

1. plan/go
2. afraid/speak
3. consider/buy
4. want/go
5. call/thank
6. willing/help
7. look forward to/return
8. learn/dance
9. recommend/buy
10. start/study

11. finish/do
12. promise/write
13. anxious/see
14. tired of/work
15. decide/go
16. like/swim
17. expect/return
18. suggest/leave
19. intend/do
20. worry about/lose

EXERCISE 43.1 | Forming Gerund Phrases

Use the words in parentheses as the basis for forming a gerund phrase to be used as the subject or object of the verb or preposition.

1. *Driving a car on long trips* can be very tiresome. *(drive/car/long trips)*
2. .... was his mistake. *(not/study)*
3. .... was her responsibility. *(prepare/food/party)*
4. She suggested .... *(invite/Aunt Ellie/dinner/Saturday)*
5. He doesn't see as well as he used to, and he's somewhat .... *(afraid of/drive/night)*
6. .... can be important in language study. *(listen/tapes)*
7. .... is prohibited. *(smoke/this section/airplane)*
8. Did you enjoy ....? *(meet/friend/Japan)*
9. I'm very fond of .... *(swim/hike/play tennis/summertime)*
10. .... can be embarrassing. *(talk/out loud/yourself)*
11. Everyone is afraid of .... *(make/mistake/new job)*
12. ....always makes me very angry. *(wait/hours/someone)*
13. The professor finished .... *(write/new textbook/few weeks ago)*
14. .... or .... is necessary to maintain good health. *(swim/two hours/every day), (take/some other/kind/exercise)*
15. I like ...., ... and .... *(walk/beach), (get out/sun), (smell/salt air)*

EXERCISE 44.1 | Using *there* in Subject Position

Change these sentences using *there* in subject position.

Example: A lamp was on the table.
            There was a lamp on the table.

1. Fourteen students were in class today.
2. A castle was on the top of the hill.
3. Some wine was in the bottle.
4. Two men were working on the problem.
5. Some red flowers were in bloom in the garden.
6. A new dress shop will be opening here soon.
7. Two boys were hiking in the woods.
8. Several people were picnicking by the river.

Exercises for Section 11

EXERCISE 45.1 | Word Order of Noun Modifiers

Use the words at the left in the correct order in the sentence.

1. new / a / large / brick
   They live in …… …… …… …… house.

2. old / leather / an / brown
   She was wearing …… …… …… …… coat.

3. steel / big / a / new
   We crossed …… …… …… …… bridge.

4. beautiful / another / silk / new
   She bought …… …… …… …… dress.

5. little / interesting / two / Japanese
   The girl was carrying …… …… …… …… dolls.

6. Boston / old / two / ugly
   Joe has slept in …… …… …… …… hotels.

7. country / quiet / little / that
   Mr. Hillum returned to …… …… …… …… retreat.

8. long / morning / my / usual
   I didn't see him today on …… …… …… …… walk.

9. Christmas / English / the / traditional
   She served …… …… …… …… pudding.

136   GRAMMAR AND DRILLBOOK

EXERCISE 46.1 | Noun Compounds and Nominal Phrases

In these sentences use a *noun* inn the blank space if it is part of a noun compound. If it is not, fill the blank with *one* or *ones*.

Examples: Does she have a flower garden or a vegetable garden?
She has a flower *garden*.

Do they live in a big house or a small house?
They live in a small *one*.

1. Do you eat in the living room or the dining room?
We eat in the dining ....
2. Are you going to construct a brick building or a stone building?
We're going to build a brick ....
3. Were those men cave dwellers or tree dwellers?
They were cave ....
4. Are those wild horses or tame horses?
They're wild ....
5. Would you prefer to live in a warm area or a cold area?
I'd prefer to live in a warm ....
6. Are those cooking utensils or eating utensils?
They're cooking ....
7. Are you going to the dress shop or the shoe shop?
I'm going to the shoe ....
8. Are they going on a camping trip or on a hunting trip?
They're going on a camping ....
9. Is that an ancient painting or a modern painting?
That's an ancient ....
10. Are those water glasses or wine glasses?
They're water ....

EXERCISE 46.2 | Noun Compounds

Answer these questions about the picture. Use noun compounds in every answer.

1. What's on the stove? — A frying pan.
2. What's on the kitchen table next to the salad bowl? ....
3. Where are the napkins? ....
4. What else is there? ....
5. What is Mrs. Jones putting on the salad? ....
6. Where does she keep the cookies? ....
7. What's in the sink? ....
8. What's broken? ....
9. What's under the sugar bowl? ....
10. What's on TV now? ....
11. Where's the baby? ....
12. What's he playing with? ....
13. What's above the toaster? ....

Exercises for Section 12

EXERCISE 47.1 | Punctuation of Words in a Series

Write answers to the questions. In each answer list three or more things that you can eat, buy, see, etc.

1. What do you usually eat for lunch?
2. What kinds of things can you buy in a department store?
3. What are some of the most interesting things to see in your country?
4. What are your favorite sports?
5. What kinds of things do you like to do?

EXERCISE 47.2 | Using *neither...nor*

Write sentences with *neither...nor* using the words that are given and any other words you want or need to use to make a complete sentence.

Examples: Tom - Bill   help
  Neither Tom nor Bill would help me.
  She said, "Neither Tom nor Bill could help us with the problem."
  Neither Tom nor Bill was willing to try to help us.

1. Margaret - June — tell
2. he — drink - smoke
3. Barbara - Harriet — coffee
4. Mr. White - Mr. Smith — attend
5. they — speak - understand
6. the clothing store - the department store — have (*or* sell)
7. the old man — see - hear
8. Jim - Bob — ask
9. the history course — interesting - useful
10. she — bread - cookies

EXERCISE 48.1 | Restating Sentences with Conjunctions

Restate these sentences omitting words when required.

1. She was laughing and she was crying at the same time.
   She was laughing and crying at the same time.
2. He likes to swim, he likes to dance, and he likes to play tennis.
3. You should either come on time or you should not come at all.
4. He was big and he was heavy.
5. You must stand up and you must fight for your principles.
6. She looked the word up in the dictionary and she told us how to pronounce it.
7. The building was modern, the building was functional, and the building was beautiful.

EXERCISE 49.1 | Practice with Conjunctions

A. Use *and* or *but* to join the two sentences. Use whichever seems more logical. Do not omit words.

1. I drink coffee. I don't drink tea.
   I drink coffee, but I don't drink tea.
2. He likes history. He likes mathematics.
3. The problem was hard. It wasn't impossible.
4. He was angry. He was not violent.
5. She was tall. She was very attractive.
6. She likes Charles. She doesn't like his friends.
7. He works hard all day. He works hard all night.
8. He was tired. He wasn't very sleepy.

B. Do the sentences again. Omit the subject and verb of the second sentence and make any other changes necessary.

1. I drink coffee. I don't drink tea.
   I drink coffee, but not tea.

EXERCISE 49.2 | Sentence Completion: Practice with Conjunctions

Complete these sentences in any logical way.

1. Both the pen ...
   Both the pen and pencil are mine.
2. Neither the teacher ...
3. He was short and ...
4. I'll see you either ...
5. I take cream but ...
6. He laughed and ...
7. I got to the bus stop on time but ...
8. We had neither time ...
9. Did Tom or ...
10. I like both ...
11. You may study either ...
12. I can speak ...
13. John promised ...

EXERCISE 50.1 | Subject and Verb Agreement

Use *was* or *were* in the blanks.

1. The news .... very bad.
2. People .... running toward the accident.
3. .... your family able to be there?
4. Neither Johnny nor Billy .... very healthy.
5. A number of children .... crying.
6. The number of children there .... quite small.
7. Both my older brother and my younger brother .... married.
8. Neither boy .... able to come.
9. There .... a number of people at the lecture.
10. The number of writers at the lecture .... surprising.

SECTION 13

Adjectives Used as Nominals
Appositives
Infinitives and Gerunds with Different Meanings after Certain Verbs
Compound Modifiers Using Numbers
Noun Phrase + Infinitive

51 Adjectives Used as Nominals

- An adjective used with the determiner *the* can function as a noun phrase. When such adjectives refer to people, they refer to all people having certain characteristics and take a plural verb.

     Do *the rich* always give to *the poor?*
     Only *the brave were* willing to go.

- When an adjective with *the* refers to an abstract quality it takes a singular verb.

     The cheapest is not always *the best.*
     The good in people *was* what the author was writing about.

  This use of the adjective should not be confused with an adjective used as a noun phrase substitute. Compare these two sentences. Notice the verb number.

     We looked over the tomatoes carefully. *The best were* sent to the fair.
     (= the best tomatoes)

     The best is just good enough for my family.
     (= an abstract quality)

- The names of colors are frequently used as NPs. They do not have to be used with the word *the.*

     Blue is my favorite color. I especially like *the blue* of sunny skies.
     In his paintings he always uses lots of *yellows* and *reds.*

EXERCISE 51.1 | Adjectives Used as Nominals. See page 167.

> Extra Drill 51.1

52 Appositives

> **Study these sentences.**
>
> His daughter, June, is a good friend of mine.
> George, my oldest son, is an engineer.
> Dr. Jones, a famous scientist, is lecturing tonight.
> A famous actress, Anita Loring, was born here.
> He drives a Toyota, a small Japanese car.
> At noon we arrived in Gloucester, a small fishing village.

- When two noun phrases are used together, and when they name the same person or thing, we say they are in *apposition*.

    Steve, my brother, is an engineer.

  The second NP *(my brother)* is called *an appositive*. It refers to the same person *(Steve)*. An appositive adds information about the first noun phrase.

  Extra Drill 52.1

- An appositive can result from omitting the words *who* or *which* and the verb *BE* from certain relative clauses.

    John, who is my brother, told me. ⟹ John, my brother, told me.

    Guatemala, *which is* a Central American country, exports coffee.

    ⟹ Guatemala, a Central American country, exports coffee.

- In speech there is usually a little pause before and after the appositive.

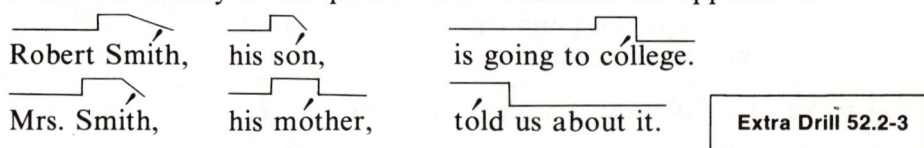

Robert Smith,   his son,   is going to college.
Mrs. Smith,   his mother,   told us about it.

Extra Drill 52.2-3

PRACTICE

Change the sentences to appositive phrases and use them in new sentences.

1. *July Fourth* is a *national holiday* in the United States.
   In the U.S. everyone celebrates *July Fourth, a national holiday.*
2. *Guatemala* is a *very interesting country.*
   Guatemala, a very interesting country, is in Central America.
3. *Dacron* is *a synthetic material.*
   My suit is made of ...., ...
4. *Steve* is *my older brother.*
   ...., ..., lives in New York.
5. *Cellulose* is *a woody material.*
   ...., ... is found in all plants.
6. I received *a nice gift.* It was *a beautiful gold watch.*
   My parents gave me ...., ...
7. *Jim* is coming tomorrow. He's *a good friend of mine.*
   I want you to meet ...., ...
8. In the woods we saw *an animal.* It was *a large deer.*
   ...., ..., was coming toward us.

EXERCISE 52.1| Making Clauses from Appositives. See page 167.

- In writing, commas are used to set off the appositive. At the end of a sentence, of course, a period is used.

   Kim, a Korean student, lived with them for a year.
   I'd like you to meet Miss Johnson, my secretary.

   With some appositives, such as the following, no pause and no commas are found.

   my brother Bob   the word "appositive"

   Extra Drill 52.4-5

- Notice the different kinds of appositives in these two sentences.

   That book is about Washington, the first President of the U.S.

   This book is about Washington the farmer; it doesn't deal with his military or political career. (Washington the soldier and politician.)

EXERCISE 52.2| Forming and Punctuating Appositives. See page 167.
EXERCISE 52.2| Changing Sentences with Appositives to the Passive. See page 168.

53 Infinitives and Gerunds with Different Meanings after Certain Verbs

- As we have seen, there are a number of verbs which can be followed by either a gerund or an infinitive with little or no difference in meaning.

    It *began to rain*.   We *continued to read*.
    It *began raining*.   We *continued reading*.

- After a few verbs in English, however, a different meaning is expressed by a gerund or an infinitive. Four of these verbs are: *forget, remember, stop* and *try*. Here is an example, using the verb *stop*.

    (1) John *stopped to see* me.
    (2) John *stopped seeing* me.

    In example (1) the infinitive *to see* is used as an infinitive of purpose. That is, we can say *John stopped in order to see me*. John was walking or driving somewhere, and he stopped at my house for the purpose of seeing me.

    In example (2) the gerund *seeing* is an NP used as the direct object of the verb "stop." This example means that John used to see me, and then he stopped. He doesn't see me anymore now.

    Extra Drill 53.1-2

- Study these examples which use the verb *remember*.

    (1) I *remembered to tell* Helen.
    (2) I *remembered telling* Helen.

    The meaning of the two sentences is quite different. Sentence (1) means that I didn't forget to tell Helen; I remembered doing it. Sentence (2) means that I remembered, or recalled, that I told Helen something; I remembered the action of telling her.

    Extra Drill 53.3-4

- *Forget* follows the idea of remember.

    I *forgot to tell*... = I didn't remember to tell...
    I *forgot telling*... = I didn't remember that I had told...

- *Try* also has two different meanings. Study these examples:

    (1) The company *tried to build* a faster airplane, but the project was too difficult.
    (2) The company *tried building* a faster airplane as a way to increase their sales.

    In the second example, building the airplane was done for another purpose—that is, to see if sales would increase.

    EXERCISE 53.1| Practice with Verbs *remember/stop/try/forget*. See page 168.

54 Compound Modifiers Using Numbers

- There is a kind of noun modifier consisting of a number and a singular noun—never a plural form. In writing, a hyphen (-) is used between the number and the noun.

    a *four-door* car   twenty *ten-cent* stamps
    a *six-day* trip   two *eight-pound* babies

Extra Drill 54.1-2

PRACTICE

1. The *drive* took *six hours* in all.
   It was a *six-hour drive*.
2. The *box of candy* weighed *two pounds*.
   It was a ....
3. The *boat* measured *forty feet* in length.
   It was a ....
4. That *building* had *ten stories*.
   It was a ....
5. The *book* had *five hundred pages*.
   It was a ....

EXERCISE 54.1 | Compound Modifiers Using Numbers. See page 169.

EXERCISE 54.2 | Compound Modifiers Using Numbers. See page 169.

55 Noun Phrase + Infinitive

- Infinitives (*to* + base form) are often used to modify noun phrases in English. They follow the modified NP. Various meanings, such as purpose or necessity, are expressed by this combination of words.

    He gave me *a book to read*. (Purpose: to read the book)
    She has *some clothes to mend*.
    I find *nothing to complain about*.

Extra Drill 55.1-2

> **PRACTICE**
>
> 1. I like *to read books.*
>   Do you have any good *books to read?*
> 2. I like *to eat fruit.*
>   Do you have any good ....?
> 3. I like *to play records.*
>   Do you have any good ....?
> 4. I like *to play games.*
>   Do you have any good ....?

Extra Drill 55.3-4

- The meaning of a noun phrase + infinitive can be expressed in other ways.

    I have a good book to read.   (a book that I want to read)
    She has clothes to mend.   (clothes that she should mend)
    He has a meeting to attend.   (a meeting that he must attend)

EXERCISE 55.1| Using the Infinitive of Purpose. See page 170.
EXERCISE 55.2| Writing Sentences with Noun + Infinitive. See page 170.

SECTION 14

Participles as Noun Modifiers: "-ing" Form
"-ing" Forms as True Adjectives
Participles as Noun Modifiers "-ed" Form
Contrast of "-ing" and "-ed" Forms

56 Participles as Nominal Modifiers: *-ing* Form

- The **-ing** forms of many intransitive verbs are used before nouns as modifiers. The **-ing** form is usually called the *present participle* (*running, working*, etc.).

    The firemen ran into the *burning building*.
    Many *working wives* have no children.

> ### PRACTICE
>
> 1. The *building* was *burning*.
>   People ran from the *burning building*.
> 2. The *bell* was *ringing*.
>   The .... made a lot of noise.
> 3. The *children* were *sleeping*.
>   We were careful not to waken the ....
> 4. The *boys* are *growing*.
>   .... eat a lot.
> 5. The *water* was *boiling*.
>   His mother kept the little boy away from the ....
> 6. The *car* was *moving*.
>   I almost fell out of the ....

Normally the noun is spoken with stronger stress than the modifier.

    bóiling wàter   crýing chìld   chánging clìmate | Extra Drill 56.1-2 |

- Many *noun compounds* are similar in form, but they have stronger stress on the first word.

    drìnking wàter   wàlking shòes   wrìting pàper | Extra Drill 56.3 |

- If the present participle (**-ing** form) has an object or complement, or is followed by a prepositional phrase or other modifier, then it must follow the noun.

PRACTICE

Use the -ing phrase in the second sentence to modify the italicized noun in the first sentence.

1. That *man* is Mr. Wells.
   He's waiting in the office.
   That man waiting in the office is Mr. Wells.

2. That young *man* is a tailor.
   He's making my suit.
   ....

3. That young *lady* is an artist.
   She's sketching the native costumes.
   ....

4. Those *women* are from Guatemala.
   They're weaving beautiful textiles.
   ....

5. Do you know that *man*?
   He's making language tapes.
   ....

6. Is that your blue *car*?
   It's standing in the middle of the street.
   ....

- The **-ing** form as a noun modifier results from omitting the words *who, which* or *that* and the verb *be* from certain relative clauses. Study these examples.

   the water *which is* boiling on the stove ⇒ the water boiling on the stove

   the baby *who's* crying in his sleep ⇒ the baby crying in his sleep

   Extra Drill 56.4

- If the **-ing** form is without an object or complement, then it is usually placed before the noun.

   the water *which is* boiling ⇒ the boiling water

   the baby *who's* crying ⇒ the crying baby

   boys *who are* growing ⇒ growing boys

   Extra Drill 56.5

- Many **-ing** forms used as modifiers come from the simple present verb forms. Study these examples:

>   The example *that follows* ⇒ the following example
>   a problem *that continues* ⇒ a continuing problem
>   wives *who work* ⇒ working wives

> Extra Drill 56.6

EXERCISE 56.1| Participles as Noun Modifiers. See page 171.

57 *-ing* Forms as True Adjectives

- We know that adjectives can modify nouns, and we have just seen that present participles can modify nouns. Is there any difference between them? Yes, there is. A true adjective can be modified by *an intensifier*. An intensifier is one of the words like *very, rather, quite, fairly, somewhat, terribly, awfully*.

>   very good   rather nice   quite old   fairly large
>   somewhat important   terribly angry   awfully hard

Most present participles cannot be modified by intensifiers. That is, we cannot say *very singing, quite waiting, rather burning*. They can, however, be modified by manner adverbs: *rapidly boiling*.

Another difference is that true adjectives can be used after *BE* and linking verbs.

>   Your sister *looks nice*.
>   This *is important*.

Most present participles cannot be used in this position. We cannot say, for example, "He seems waiting," or "She looks running."

- There are, however, quite a few present participles that are adjectives in every way. They can be modified by intensifiers, they can be used after linking verbs, and they can be compared by using *more* or *most*. *Interesting* is one of these words.

>   A *very interesting* movie was shown.
>   The program *was interesting*.
>   This book is *more interesting than* that one.

There is no rule which tells which *-ing* forms can be used like true adjectives. They have to be learned through practice and experience. All the present participles in the list below can be used as true adjectives. They express feeling or mental state. (For a more complete list, see the appendix, page 202.)

> Extra Drill 57.1

amazing	boring	exciting	pleasing
amusing	charming	frightening	puzzling
annoying	convincing	interesting	satisfying
appealing	disappointing	knowing	surprising
astonishing	entertaining	loving	tiring

PRACTICE

Substitute progressively.

SUBJECT	VERB	INTENSIFIER	PRESENT PARTICIPLE
The movie	is	very	interesting.

TEACHER	STUDENT
Past	The movie was very interesting.
rather	....
amusing	....
Yes/No Question	....
quite	....
disappointing	....
Affirmative Statement	....
the book	....
somewhat	....
very	....
entertaining	....
Negative Statement	....
the speaker	....
convincing	The speaker wasn't very convincing.

EXERCISE 57.1 | Practice with *-ing* Forms. See page 172.

58 Participles as Nominal Modifiers: *-ed* Form

- The **-ed** form of a verb is the form that is used with *have* or *has* to form verb phrases such as *have worked, has seen,* etc. Another name for this form is *past participle*. Many past participles, as you know, are irregular (*broken, seen,* etc.).

- Past participles are also used before nouns as modifiers.

    a *broken* watch   the *burned* papers   *finished* work

Extra Drill 58.1

> ## PRACTICE
>
> 1. The *food* had *spoiled*.
>   We threw away all the *spoiled food*.
> 2. The child's *toy* has *broken*.
>   What can you do with a ....?
> 3. This *magazine* has been *torn*.
>   I can't read this ....
> 4. The three *children* had become *lost*.
>   All the men have gone to look for the ....
> 5. The *money* was *borrowed* from me.
>   I asked him to repay the .... to me.
> 6. Some *food* is *frozen*
>   My mother always buys ....

Extra Drill 58.2

- If the past participle is followed by a prepositional phrase, then it must follow the noun.

    My money was with the *papers burned in the fire.*

- Like a present participle, most past participles cannot be used as true adjectives. That is, they are not used with intensifiers, and they cannot be compared by using *more* or *most*.

    There are some, however, that are like true adjectives. Again these must be learned. The list below shows those formed from verbs you have learned to use. (For a more complete list, see the appendix, page 203.)

amazed	charmed	excited	tired
amused	confused	interested	troubled
annoyed	crowded	pleased	worried
astonished	disappointed	puzzled	
bored	encouraged	satisfied	

SECTION FOURTEEN

PRACTICE

Substitute progressively.

SUBJECT	VERB	INTENSIFIER	PAST PARTICIPLE
The girl	is	rather	tired.

TEACHER	STUDENT
Past	The girl was rather tired.
confused	....
worried	....
somewhat	....
very	....
Negative Statement	....
disappointed	....
Affirmative Statement	....
encouraged	....
Present	....
tired	....
rather	The girl's rather tired.

PRACTICE

Substitute progressively.

	INTENSIFIER	PAST PARTICIPLE	ADJECTIVE	NOUN
He's a	very	troubled	young	man.

TEACHER	STUDENT
annoyed	He's a very annoyed young man.
confused	....
somewhat	....
terribly	....
worried	....
rather	....
puzzled	....

- The past participle as a noun modifier results from deleting the words *who, which* or *that* and the verb *BE* from certain relative clauses.

a language *which is* spoken by millions ⟹ a language spoken by millions

a president *who was* elected by the people ⟹ a president elected by the people

a man *who hadn't been* chosen by the people ⟹ a man not chosen by the people

the papers *which were* not burned ⟹ the papers not burned

> **Extra Drill 58.3-5**

- If the past participle occurs without a complement, then it is usually placed before the noun.

   The building *which was* burned ⟹ the burned building

   a scientist *who was* trained ⟹ a trained scientist

> **Extra Drill 58.6-8**

EXERCISE 58.1 | *-ing* and *-ed* Verb Forms Used as True Adjectives. See page 172.
EXERCISE 58.2 | Progressive Addition of Appositives and Other Modifiers. See page 173.

59 Contrast of *-ing* and *-ed* Forms

- The meaning of present and past participles used as noun modifiers is different. If the participles are formed from *intransitive verbs*, the difference is between an action taking place at the present time and one that has been completed.

   PRESENT ACTION: the *falling* tree   (the tree is falling now)
   COMPLETED ACTION: the *fallen* tree   (the tree has already fallen)

If the participles are formed from *transitive verbs*, the present participle is active in meaning and the past participle is passive in meaning.

   ACTIVE: the *amusing* girl   (the girl herself is amusing)
   PASSIVE: the *amused* girl   (the girl was amused by someone else)
   ACTIVE: the *hunting* animal   (the animal itself is hunting something)
   PASSIVE: the *hunted* animal   (the animal is being hunted by something)

- The *-ing* and *-ed* forms which function as true adjectives can be used after *BE* and linking verbs.

  In general, these participles are formed from verbs that require animate objects.

  The speech *disappointed* me.
  The speech was *disappointing*.
  I was *disappointed*.

  The dinner *satisfied* everyone.
  The dinner seemed *satisfying*.
  They seemed *satisfied*.

> **Extra Drill 59.1**

PRACTICE

Answer the questions in accordance with the statement of fact.

	STATEMENT OF FACT		
1.	The voice on the telephone puzzled Jean	Who was puzzled?	Jean was.
2.	The lecture bored everyone.	What was boring?	The lecture was.
3.	The play amused Tom.	What was amusing?	....
4.	His actions astonished everyone.	Who was astonished?	....
5.	Her story convinced the jurors.	What was convincing?	....
6.	The story frightened the children.	Who was frightened?	....

EXERCISE 59.1 | Single Word *-ing* and *-ed* Modifiers. See page 174.

EXERCISE 59.2 | Using *-ing* and *-ed* Modifiers. See page 174.

SECTION 15

Verbs Followed by Two Objects: Indirect Object with "to"
Verbs Followed by Two Objects: Indirect Object with "for"
Verbs Followed by Two Objects: Fixed Order
Verbs Followed by an Infinitive with Subject
Verbs Followed by a Base Form with Subject

---

60 Verbs Followed by Two Objects: Indirect Object with *to*

- There are some transitive verbs in English which can take two objects. One of the objects is called the *direct object*. The other is called the *indirect object*. An **indirect object** names the person for whom the action of the verb is performed.

	INDIRECT OBJECT	DIRECT OBJECT
We gave	**Bob**	*a book.*
He lent	**me**	*some money.*
I wrote	**Susan**	*a letter.*
They mailed	**us**	*some gifts.*

- The preposition **to** is often used to emphasize the indirect object. In this case, the direct object comes before the prepositional phrase.

	DIRECT OBJECT	INDIRECT OBJECT
We gave	*a book*	**to Bob.**
They mailed	*some gifts*	**to us.**

Extra Drill 60.1-3

- If the direct object is an object pronoun (usually *it* or *them*), the indirect object is always expressed by a prepositional phrase.

  We gave *it* **to Bob.**
  They mailed *them* **to us.**

Extra Drill 60.4-5

- These are some of the transitive verbs which can take two objects. All of them can use **to** with the indirect object. (For a more complete list, see the appendix, page 201.)

bring	pay	sing
give	read	take
lend	sell	teach
mail	send	tell
offer	show	write

PRACTICE

Use the cue words in the answer. Substitute pronouns for NPs whenever appropriate.

	SPEAKER A	SPEAKER B
1.	What did he give you? *(a watch)*	He gave me a watch.
	When did he give it to you? *(yesterday)*	He gave it to me yesterday.
2.	What did Bill bring Mary? *(some flowers)*	He brought her some flowers.
	When did he bring them to her? *(this morning)*	He brought them to her this morning.
3.	What did Jack lend Lee? *(some money)*	....
	When did he lend it to him? *(a few days ago)*	....
4.	What did Mrs. Wells send her daughter? *(a dress)*	....
	When did she send it to her? *(last week)*	....
5.	What did Tom sell Roger? *(his bike)*	....
	When did he sell it to him? *(last month)*	....

Extra Drill 60.6-8

61 Verbs Followed by Two Objects: Indirect Object with *for*

- Some indirect objects are introduced by **for** instead of **to**. The use of *for* generally means that an action is performed for the benefit of someone.

> Mrs. Wells made *a dress* **for her daughter**.
> He bought *a house* **for his family**.

- The indirect object may precede the direct object if the direct object is not an object pronoun.

> Mrs. Wells made **her daughter** *a dress*.   She made **it for her**.
> He bought **his family** *a house*.   He bought **it for them**.

Extra Drill 61.1-2

156 GRAMMAR AND DRILLBOOK

- These are some of the transitive verbs that can be followed by two objects and which use **for** to introduce the indirect object. (For a more complete list, see the appendix, page 201.)

build	cook	make
buy	do	order
call	find	play
catch	get	save
choose	leave	sew

Extra Drill 61.3

62 Verbs Followed by Two Objects: Fixed Order

- Some transitive verbs take two objects in a fixed order only: the *direct* object always precedes the *indirect* object with preposition.

	DIRECT OBJECT	INDIRECT OBJECT
He speaks	*English*	**to me.**
I explained	*the problem*	**to Bob.**
Please keep	*this money*	**for me.**
He opened	*the door*	**for the lady.**

- These are some of the verbs of this kind. (For a more complete list, see the appendix, page 202.)

INDIRECT OBJECT WITH **TO**	INDIRECT OBJECT WITH **FOR**
explain	answer
introduce	fix
remember	keep
repeat	open
say	pronounce
speak	translate

Extra Drill 62.1

- The verb *ask,* meaning "inquire," is always followed by (1) an indirect object and then (2) a direct object.

    May I ask you a question?

  When *ask* means "request," we can use the preposition *of* with the indirect object.

    May I ask *you* a favor?
    (or) May I ask a favor *of you?*

EXERCISE 62.1 | Order of Direct and Indirect Objects. See page 175.

EXERCISE 62.2 | Verbs that Take Two Objects. See page 175.

- When the direct object is a very long phrase or clause it usually comes after shorter indirect object. This is true after all verbs not requiring fixed order (in Points 60 and 61) as well as some of the "fixed order" ones in Point 62.

  I explained *to Bob* that I had tried to reach him several times that evening.

  > I'll introduce *to you* a person who may just be able to supply you with those documents.

  > Please repeat *to the judge* the events of the morning of June 6, 1977.

  EXERCISE 62.3 | Order of Direct and Indirect Objects. See page 176.

- When sentences with transitive verbs are made passive, either the direct or indirect object may become the subject of the passive sentence in most cases.

  > ACTIVE: We gave *Mr. Johnson a watch* when he retired.
  >
  > PASSIVE:
  > (DIRECT OBJECT AS SUBJECT) *A watch* was given Mr. Johnson when he retired.
  >
  > (INDIRECT OBJECT AS SUBJECT) *Mr. Johnson* was given a watch when he retired.

  Indirect objects of "fixed order" verbs (listed under Point 62) cannot be made subject of a passive sentence.

  EXERCISE 62.4 | Verbs with Two Objects: Passive. See page 177.

63 Verbs Followed by an Infinitive with Subject

- We have studied verbs that are followed by infinitives.

  > I'd *like to go*.
  > She *wanted to buy* a suit.

  In sentences like these, the subject of the sentence is also the subject of the infinitive.

- Often the infinitive has a subject which is different from the subject of the sentence.

  > I'd like *Mary* to go.
  > She wanted *John* to buy a suit.

  > Extra Drill 63.1–3

- These are a few of the verbs which can be followed by an infinitive with a subject. (For a more complete list, see the appendix, page 199.)

advise	help	require
ask	invite	teach
assist	like	tell
cause	need	want
expect	order	would like
force	permit	
get	prefer	

Extra Drill 63.4

PRACTICE

Practice this dialog.

KAREN: Mother, guess what?

MOTHER: What?

KAREN: Bob's invited *me to go* to the school dance tonight.

MOTHER: That's nice.

KAREN: Steve has asked *Lisa to go*. And Kent has invited *Anne to go* with him. We're all going together.

MOTHER: Do you want *me to help* you dress?

KAREN: Oh, yes, please.

MOTHER: What time is the dance?

KAREN: Eight o'clock. The boys said they expected *us to be* ready at 7:30 sharp.

MOTHER: You'll have to hurry. You start doing your hair. And I'll begin getting your clothes ready.

- When it is clear what the infinitive should be, the verb (along with its object or modifiers) may be omitted. Only **to** is retained.

    Did your husband stop working?
       Yes. The doctor advised him *to*. (stop working)

    Did Tom take the car to be fixed?
       Yes. I told him *to*. (take the car to be fixed)

Extra Drill 63.5

EXERCISE 63.1 | Verb + Infinitive with Subject: Elliptical Answers. See page 178.

- Many sentences which contain a verb followed by an infinitive can be made negative in two ways: (1) the main verb can be made negative, or (2) the infinitive can be made negative by using the word *not*.

  Usually the meaning of these two negative sentences is different.

  >I advised him to go.   He will ask you to come.
  >(1) I *didn't advise* him to go.   (1) He *won't ask* you to come.
  >(2) I advised him *not to go*.   (2) He will ask you *not to come*.

  The second clearly states what my advice to him was. The first does not state what my advice to him was, and there is even the possibility that I didn't give him any advice at all.

  Furthermore, (1) is sometimes used as a polite way of phrasing the meaning of (2). This is particularly true of the verbs *advise, expect,* and *prefer* in present tense first person.

  >(1) I *don't advise* you *to go* out in this storm.
  >(2) I *advise* you *not to go* out in this storm.

Extra Drill 63.6-7

64 Verbs Followed by a Base Form with Subject

- The four verbs *make, let, have* and *help* are regularly followed by the *base form* of a verb with a subject. The subject of the base form is always a noun or an object pronoun. It is unusual for these base forms to be made negative; only the main verb is made negative.

  >The teacher had *the students read* a book.
  >John's mother made *him stay* home.
  >Won't you let *me come*?
  >Bill helped *his father wash* the car.

- The meaning of *have* in this kind of construction is "cause." *Make* means "order" or "require." *Let* and *help* are used with their basic meanings of "permit" and "assist."

- The verb *help* is different from the other three verbs *(make, let, have)* because the following verb may take **to** with no difference in meaning.

  >Bob helped *me carry* the wood.
  >Bob helped *me to carry* the wood.

PRACTICE

Substitute progressively.

SUBJECT	VERB	SUBJECT OF BASE FORM	BASE FORM
He	makes	the boys	help.

TEACHER	STUDENT
Past	He made the boys help.
let	....
try	....
Yes/No Question	....
have	....
work	....
make	....
Negative Statement	He didn't make the boys work.

- Sensory verbs, such as *see, watch, hear, listen to* and *feel* can also be followed by a base form with subject.

    We heard *the baby cry.*
    They watched *their father drive away.*
    We saw *him go.*
    I listened to *the orchestra play Mozart.*

Extra Drill 64.1-2

EXERCISE 64.1 | Summary Exercise: Verb + Infinitive/Base Form with Subject. See page 178.

SECTION 16

Verbs Followed by a Gerund with Subject
Verbs Followed by NP (Object) + NP (Complement)
Verbs Followed by NP (Object) + Adjective (Complement)
The Use of "for" + an Infinitive with Subject

---

65 Verbs Followed by a Gerund with Subject

- In sentences in which a gerund immediately follows a main verb, the subject of the main verb is also the subject of a gerund.

I like *swimming*.	(*I swim* and *I like* it.)
Susan enjoys *dancing*.	(*Susan dances* and *she likes* it.)

- Often the subject of a gerund is different from the subject of the main verb. In such a case the gerund subject appears between the main verb and the gerund.

I resent *their asking*.	(*They ask* and *I resent* it.)
We talked about *Bill leaving*.	(*Bill left* and *we talked* about it.)
Mary's worried about *me smoking*.	(*I smoke* and *Mary worries* about it.)

    For a list of verbs that can be used this way see the appendix, page 199.

- The subject of a gerund must be either a possessive or possessive noun in *formal* speech and writing.

    She's worried about { my / Bill's } smoking.   **Extra Drill 65.1**

    Informal speech frequently uses an objective pronoun or noun as gerund subject.

    We talked about { him / Bill } leaving.   **Extra Drill 65.2**

- When the gerund subject is a possessive the gerund generally takes an *adjective* modifier; with a noun or objective pronoun an *adverbial* modifier is used.

    She's worried about *my excessive smoking*.
    She's worried about *me smoking excessively*.

> ## PRACTICE
>
> **Answer the questions.**
>
> **A. Use Noun + Gerund**
>
> 1. Her father smokes.
>   What is Mary worried about?   She's worried about her father smoking.
>
> 2. Her son flies an airplane.
>   What is Mrs. White concerned about?   . . . .
>
> 3. People ask him personal questions.
>   What does Charles resent?   . . . .
>
> **B. Use Possessive Pronoun + Gerund**
>
> 1. Mary sings.
>   What do we enjoy?   We enjoy her singing.
>
> 2. Mr. Chase drives too fast.
>   What is his wife worried about?   . . . .
>
> 3. John makes fun of her.
>   What does Mary dislike?   . . . .

EXERCISE 65.1| Using Gerunds. See page 179.

EXERCISE 65.2| Practice with Verbs Followed by Gerund with Subject. See page 180.

> **Extra Drill 65.3**

66 Verbs followed by NP (Object) and NP (Complement)

- After a few transitive verbs it is possible to use two noun phrases which refer to the same person or thing. The first NP is used as an object, the other as a complement of the object with the optional verb *BE* omitted.

> We elected *Mr. Thomas president.*
> (= We elected *Mr. Thomas to be president.*)
>
> Everyone believed *him a good leader.*
> (= Everyone believed *him to be a good leader.*)

- These are some of the verbs that can be followed by two noun phrases:

believe	consider	name
call	elect	suppose
choose	make	think

> **Extra Drill 66.1**

SECTION SIXTEEN 163

PRACTICE

1. He's called Billy.
   We call *him Billy*.
2. Spelling is a problem.
   I consider *it a problem*.
3. Mr. Wall is president.
   We elected *him president*.
4. Mr. Jones is the secretary.
   We named ....
5. Helen's my best friend.
   I consider ....
6. The dance was a success.
   Everyone thought ....
7. New York is my home.
   I've made ....
8. Silk-making was a secret of the Chinese.
   The Chinese considered ....

67 Verbs followed by NP (Object) + Adjective (Complement)

- Some transitive verbs can be followed by a direct object and an adjective or past participle as complement of the object.

   She made *me happy*.
   I kept *them amused*.
   She considers *her students intelligent*.

- These are some of the verbs of this kind:

believe	get	make
call	imagine	prefer
consider	keep	prove
feel	leave	think
find	like	want

Extra Drill 67.1

> **PRACTICE**
>
> 1. Jim's intelligent.
>   The teachers all consider *him intelligent.*
> 2. The examination was too hard.
>   We thought it *too hard.*
> 3. The tea was too sweet.
>   I don't like ....
> 4. The costumes were charming.
>   Everyone thought ....
> 5. Mr. Wells was wrong.
>   We all considered ....
> 6. Bob's helpful.
>   We've always found ....
> 7. The used car dealer seemed to be dishonest.
>   I felt ....

Extra Drill 67.2

EXERCISE 67.1 | Forming Sentences with NP (Object) + NP or Adjective (Complement). See page 182.

68 The Use of *for* + an Infinitive with Subject

- We have seen that certain verbs may be followed by an infinitive with subject.

    He wanted *me to come.*
    We asked *them to help.*

- After *BE* and linking verbs an infinitive with subject may follow a complement of the verb. In this case, the word *for* is used before the subject of the infinitive.

    It's easy *for you to say* that.
    She was anxious *for John to meet* her sister.
    It didn't seem necessary *for us to be* there.
    It'll be a shame *for her to leave.*

Extra Drill 68.1

PRACTICE

1. Barbara thinks Bob should read the book.
   She thinks it's important *for him to read the book.*
2. Mrs. Chase wants us to come.
   She believes it's necessary *for us to come.*
3. Mr. Wells wants us to be there.
   He seems quite anxious . . . .
4. Mr. Young thinks his students should study.
   He says it's time . . . .
5. Mr. and Mrs. Forest would like Jim to come anytime.
   They'd be glad . . . .
6. Mrs. Ward wants her husband to buy a new car.
   She's anxious . . . .

PRACTICE

Change the sentences. Begin your new sentence with it.

1. For us to come tomorrow is impossible.
   It's impossible for us to come tomorrow.
2. For me to advise you would be very difficult.
   . . . .
3. For them to go would be most foolish.
   . . . .
4. For you to find out the answer that way will be hard.
   . . . .
5. For Mr. Caldwell to go up today might be dangerous.
   . . . .

EXERCISE 68.1 | Forming Questions Using *for* + Infinitive with Subject. See page 182.
EXERCISE 68.2 | Summary Exercise: Verb + Gerund/Infinitive/Base Form with Subject. See page 183.
EXERCISE 68.3 | Summary Exercise: Verb + Gerund/Infinitive/Base Form with Subject. See page 183.

EXERCISES FOR SECTIONS 13-16

Exercises for Section 13

EXERCISE 51.1 | Adjectives Used as Nominals

Fill in the blanks with the present tense form of one of the verbs from the list or with the verb *BE*. Use a plural verb if the sentence subject refers to people, use singular if it refers to an abstraction.

    become   lack   survive
    find   learn

Example: The young *learn* from the old.

1. The desired .... not always desirable.
2. The Swiss .... famous watchmakers.
3. Only the fittest .... to maturity.
4. The unusual too often .... common.
5. The latest .... that the President won't go to Europe.
6. The unemployed .... it very hard to get back on their feet.
7. The Irish .... full of sentimental beliefs.
8. The simple .... often the most beautiful.

EXERCISE 52.1 | Making Clauses from Appositives

Read the sentences, making a clause from the appositive. Use *who* or *which* to begin the clause.

Example: My brother Jack, *an architect,* helped us draw plans for the house.
My brother Jack, *who's an architect,* helped us draw plans for the house.

1. I'd like you to meet Mr. Jones, a friend of mine.
2. I told him all about Teheran, my home for two years.
3. Aunt Jane, my mother's sister, got married last month.
4. That bridge was built by Robert Thomas, one of the most famous engineers in the world.
5. His suit is made of dacron, one of the best synthetic materials.
6. Mr. Long, our country's ambassador to Australia, has been there for six years.
7. Basketball, a very fast game, was invented by a Canadian.

EXERCISE 52.2 | Forming and Punctuating Appositives

A. Expand the sentences so that each contains a noun appositive.

Examples: James is a good student.
James, his son, is a good student.
James, a good student, studies hard every night.
James, the son of a famous scientist, is a good student.

1. Helen is a nurse.
2. Morocco is a North African country.
3. Japanese is a language spoken by millions.
4. Edison is the inventor of the electric light.
5. Peru is a country in South America.
6. Montreal is an important city in Canada.
7. Shrimp is a kind of seafood.

B. Write five sentences of your own which include an appositive.

EXERCISE 52.3 | Changing Sentences with Appositives to the Passive
Change the sentences to the passive.
Example: Dr. Smith, a famous archaeologist, wrote this book.
   This book was written by Dr. Smith, a famous archaeologist.

1. Henry Long, the famous photographer, took those unusual pictures.
2. Mr. Steel, our architect, designed those buildings.
3. Dr. Watts, a famous scientist, has made an important discovery.
4. Elizabeth Conrad, a modern novelist, wrote that book.
5. Dr. Dale, a professor at the university, will give the lecture.
6. Dr. Short, a famous archaeologist, discovered those valuable objects.

EXERCISE 53.1 | Practice with Verbs *remember/stop/try/forget*
Complete the following sentences by using the infinitive or gerund of the verb, whichever is appropriate to the meaning of the sentence.

(visit)   1. Was that Miss Love who just left?
          Yes, she stops .... me every day.

(mail)   2. Did you mail my letter?
          Yes, you know I never forget .... letters.

(write)   3. What do you hear from the Johnsons?
          Nothing at all. We stopped .... to each other two years ago.

(promise)   4. Don't forget you promised to take me out to dinner.
          I don't remember .... that.

(forget)   5. Do you remember when we each lost $100 on the horse races?
          Don't remind me. I've been trying .... it all these years.

(call)   6. I hope you called Jean and Helen as you promised.
          Well, I remembered .... Jean but I forgot .... Helen.

(rain)   7. Are we going to have the picnic?
          Yes, it's stopped ...., thank goodness.

(go)	8.	I hope you remembered .... to the bank.
		Oh, my gosh! I forgot .... there.
(close)	9.	This door is awfully big and heavy.
		Do you want me to help you try .... it?
(close)	10.	It's too noisy in here. I can't study.
		Neither can I. Let's try .... the door.
(invite)	11.	Wasn't that Mrs. Lattimer who just left?
		Yes, she stopped .... us to dinner.
(take)	12.	The library called about the two overdue books you have.
		They're wrong! I remember .... them back last week.

EXERCISE 54.1 | Compound Modifiers Using Numbers

Change the sentences, making the clause into a compound modifier preceding the noun.

Example: He gave her a box of candy that weighed two pounds.
He gave her a two-pound box of candy.

1. He was carrying a sack of rice that weighed fifty pounds.
2. Our teacher gave us an exam that lasted two hours.
3. He wrote a book on astronomy that had five hundred pages.
4. They went on a trip to the moon that lasted six days.
5. They built a house that had three bedrooms.
6. They made a movie that was fifteen minutes long.
7. He bought a stamp that cost ten cents.
8. He gave a lecture that lasted for two hours.
9. They bought a house that cost fifty thousand dollars.
10. They took a rest that lasted for thirty minutes.

EXERCISE 54.2 | Compound Modifiers Using Numbers

Change the noun phrases to a structure using a compound modifier + noun. Then write an original sentence of your own using this structure.

Example: a newspaper of eight pages ⟹ *an eight-page newspaper*
Mr. Jones is the editor of an eight-page newspaper.

1. a composition of two pages
2. tickets that cost five dollars
3. a walk of five miles
4. a flight of six hours
5. a conversation of two hours
6. a suit that costs fifty dollars

EXERCISE 55.1 | Using the Infinitive of Purpose

Change these sentences into ones with an infinitive of purpose instead of an adjective clause.

1. Mr. Hamilton gave me *a letter that I must type.*
   Mr. Hamilton gave me a letter to type.
2. Here's a phone number that you should remember.
3. Bear Lake is a place where you could spend your vacation.
4. Do you have fifty dollars that you can spend on a sewing machine?
5. Jerome Collins is a man that you can trust.
6. I've got several more exercises that I must do tonight.
7. Mrs. Longacre brought some potato salad that we can eat.
8. I saw a place a mile back that we can eat at.

EXERCISE 55.2 | Writing Sentences with Noun + Infinitive

Form seven sentences using appropriate combinations of the nouns and infinitives.

Examples: I have a lot of hard *work to do* this afternoon.
When Bill has *work to do*, he always tries to get his brother to help.
If you don't have any *work to do*, let's go to the movies.

work	to do
fruit	to make
cookies	to mend
socks	to write
clothes	to take
report	to study
job	to wash
exam	to bake
experiment	to eat
geography	to give
letter	
medicine	
advice	

Exercises for Section 14

EXERCISE 56.1 | Participles as Noun Modifiers

Answer the questions with a noun phrase. Study the example.

Example: What did that look like to you?
  A falling star.

1.

What did that sound like to you?

2.

What does that sound like to you?

3.

What does that sound like to you?

4.

What does that look like to you?

5.

What does that smell like to you?

6.

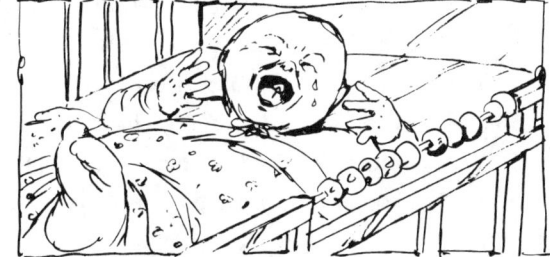

What does that sound like to you?

EXERCISE 57.1 | Practice with *-ing* Forms

Answer the question using *very* before the *-ing* forms used as true adjectives. If *very* cannot be used, reply using any appropriate adverb (e.g., with all its might). Study the examples.

1. Was the book interesting?
   Yes, it was very interesting.
2. Was the building burning?
   Yes, it was burning fiercely.   (*very* cannot be used)
3. Was the speaker convincing?
4. Is his job demanding?
5. Was the computer working?
6. Is the water boiling?
7. Were the directions confusing?
8. Was the drink refreshing?
9. Was the wind blowing?
10. Was the taste pleasing?
11. Is the bell ringing?
12. Was the letter reassuring?
13. Are the children growing?
14. Was the ride thrilling?
15. Was the experience satisfying?

EXERCISE 58.1 | *-ing* and *-ed* Verb Forms Used as True Adjectives

Read the sentence and *if it is possible,* use an intensifier (*very, rather, quite,* etc.) before the present or past participle that is italicized. If an intensifier is not possible, use one of these adverbs to modify the participle: badly, frequently, loudly, quietly, rapidly, sharply, slowly.

Examples: She's an *amazing* person.
            She's a very amazing person.
            Smoke was pouring from the *burning* building.
            Smoke was pouring from the fiercely burning building.

1. Teaching is *satisfying* work.
2. The man *hiding* in the woods ran when he saw us.
3. We watched the *disappearing* sun.
4. We had a *satisfied* look on his face.
5. She tried to quiet the *crying* children.
6. We saw some *excited* people.
7. We saw an *entertaining* play last night.

8. They cheered their *elected* leader.
9. He seemed to be a *troubled* young man.
10. He told us a *convincing* story.
11. When we finally got home, we had two *tired* boys.
12. We thought it was a *disappointing* program.
13. We took a drive through the *damaged* area.
14. I saw a *repeated* program on TV last night.
15. What can we do about *increasing* costs?

EXERCISE 58.2 | Progressive Addition of Appositives and Other Modifiers
Form sentences, each time adding a modifier or appositive to the preceding sentence.

Example: That man works for the Edison Company.
(a) tall   That tall man works for the Edison Company.
(b) standing over there   That tall man standing over there works for the Edison Company.
(c) an old manufacturing firm   That tall man standing over there works for the Edison Company, an old manufacturing firm.

1. We took a picture of a bridge.
   (a) old
   (b) interesting
   (c) stone
   (d) built in 1732
2. We have customers.
   (a) several
   (b) satisfied
   (c) very
   (d) doing business with us
3. We stayed in a hotel.
   (a) beautiful
   (b) five hundred-room
   (c) new
   (d) located in the center of the city
4. He works in an office building.
   (a) fifty-story
   (b) large
   (c) designed by Mr. Oda
   (d) a Japanese architect
   (e) educated in Sweden

EXERCISE 59.1 | Single Word -ing and -ed Modifiers

Fill the blanks with the present or past participle form of the verbs at the left.

(break)	1.	The boys ran when they saw the .... window.
(bore)	2.	It was a very .... movie.
(amuse)	3.	I thought it was a very .... story.
(tire)	4.	We had a .... trip.
(freeze)	5.	His mother buys a lot of .... foods.
(run)	6.	The house had no .... water.
(tire)	7.	The .... workers were given a short rest.
(convince)	8.	He gave a very .... argument.
(visit)	9.	Mary Jones is a .... nurse.
(continue)	10.	I don't like .... problems.
(miss)	11.	Every year there are large numbers of .... persons,
(rent)	12.	Many men now drive .... cars,
(close)	13.	I could hear them argue behind the .... door.
(worry)	14.	He was a very .... boy.
(accompany)	15.	With this lesson there is an .... tape.
(excite)	16.	I read a very .... book last night.
(speak)	17.	We are studying the .... language.
(begin)	18.	My friend is a .... English student.
(understand)	19.	They are very .... parents.
(follow)	20.	Please do the .... exercise.

EXERCISE 59.2 | Using -ing and -ed Modifiers

Use the word or words in parentheses to modify the italicized noun in the sentence. Use the present or past participle of the verb, whichever is appropriate.

Examples:

(work)	Many *wives* have no children.
	Many working wives have no children.
(bloom in the garden)	Do you like the *flowers*?
	Do you like the flowers blooming in the garden?
(puzzle)	1. The little *boy* didn't know where he was.
(confuse by all the noise)	2. The little *boy* began crying for his parents.
(dig in the garden)	3. That *woman* is becoming red in the face.
(hold the flowers)	4. That little *girl* is charming.
(astonish)	5. He told us a *story*.
(cook)	6. She put the *vegetables* on the table.

(tire)   7. We returned late from our *trip*.
(chop the tree)   8. You'd better tell that *man* to be careful.
(break)   9. Where can I can take my *watch* to be repaired?
(plant in that field) 10. The *crops* look very dry.

Exercises for Section 15

EXERCISE 62.1| Order of Direct and Indirect Objects

If it is possible, change the sentence so that the indirect object precedes the direct object.

Examples: He gave the book to me.
He gave me the book.
She showed it to us.
(The order cannot be changed)

1. They offered some money to me.
2. She sang it to us.
3. I never lend money to my friends.
4. He opened the door for her.
5. He showed it to Mr. Wilson.
6. Why didn't he say hello to me?
7. I found some nice cuff links for my brother.
8. Mr. Smith brought his raincoat to Mr. Wells.
9. I explained the math problem to him.
10. We gave a purse to my sister for her birthday.
11. She kept it for him last year.
12. I think you should write a letter to Charles tomorrow.
13. He introduced his friend to me.
14. I'll give it to you tomorrow.
15. He showed his son's picture to me.

EXERCISE 62.2| Verbs That Take Two Objects

Change the indirect object to a pronoun, and *if possible,* **use the indirect object before the direct object.**

Examples: She made a dress for Mary.
She made her a dress.
I suggested a plan to Mr. Wilson.
I suggested a plan to him.
(indirect object cannot precede.)

1. Please write a letter to Mr. Jones.
2. She bought a dress for Mary.
3. I explained the problem to Tom.
4. I always speak English to Mrs. Rodriguez.
5. Find a good book for John.
6. Please pronounce these words for Kim.
7. I made a hotel reservation for Mr. Nichols.
8. I sold my old car to Mr. Wilson.
9. Johnny closed the door for the teacher.
10. I lent some money to Ted.
11. Please keep this money for Jane.
12. I answered the question for Bill.
13. He told his story to the newspaper reporter.
14. Please remember me to your wife.
15. I introduced Mary to my friend Tom.

EXERCISE 62.3 | Order of Direct and Indirect Objects

Complete the sentence using the direct and indirect objects given. Supply "to" or "for" as needed.

1. She gave *her friend a gift of the most beautiful china she could find.*
   (her friend)
   (a gift of the most beautiful china she could find)
2. They reported ....
   (the police)
   (the robbery which took place while they were away on vacation)
3. He ordered ....
   (me)
   (a ham and cheese sandwich, a bowl of soup and a glass of milk)
4. They ordered ....
   (the hungry children they had found)
   (sandwiches)
5. Mary Wilson bought ....
   (her husband and two sons)
   (bathrobes)
6. Mrs. Avon bought ....
   (her husband)
   (a new red wool bathrobe which was on sale)

7. John built ....
   (his parents)
   (a beautiful new brick house in the best part of town)
8. Gordon Frakes gave ....
   (the school he got his engineering degree from)
   ($50,000)
9. I've sent ....
   (an old friend)
   (most of my valuable old German postage stamps from before World War I.)

EXERCISE 62.4 | Verbs with Two Objects: Passive

A. Change the sentences to the passive, using *the direct object* as the subject of the new sentence. Do not use *by + agent*.

Example: He introduced the speaker to us.
The speaker was introduced to us.

1. They offered some money to the city.
2. She will read a story to the children.
3. We sold some things to the government.
4. He gave some money to the hospital.
5. They'll give some pictures to his friends.
6. He showed a letter to the president.
7. He explained the problem to them.

B. Make the sentences passive in the same manner, but omit the indirect object.

Example: He introduced the speaker to us.
The speaker was introduced.

C. Change the following sentences to the passive, using *the indirect object* as the subject of the new sentence. Do not use *by + agent*.

1. They gave John a watch for his birthday.
   John was given a watch for his birthday.
2. They taught her English.
3. They will give you directions for getting here.
4. The bank will offer him a loan.
5. The doctor had given them shots.
6. They have not yet told him the results of his examination.

EXERCISE 63.1 | Verb + Infinitive with Subject: Elliptical Answers
Use the cue verb in answering the question. Study the examples.

1. Did your husband stop working? *(advise)*
   Yes, { the doctor / I / everyone } advised him to.
2. Did Tom take the car to be fixed? *(tell)*
   Yes, { I / his father / his wife } told him to.
3. Did Mary go to the grocery store? *(ask)*
4. Is her husband going to change jobs? *(want)*
5. Is your son taking chemistry in college? *(require)*
6. Did Fulton move his car from in front of the school? *(order)*
7. Is your daughter getting married soon? *(would like)*

EXERCISE 64.1 | Summary Exercise: Verb + Infinitive / Base Form with Subject
Substitute the cued main verbs. Use the infinitive or base form of *go* as required.

1. advise   We advised Bob to go.
2. let   We let Bob go.
3. watched   ....
4. made   ....
5. ordered   ....
6. heard   ....
7. asked   ....
8. told   ....
9. had   ....
10. permitted   ....
11. saw   ....
12. expected   ....

Exercises for Section 16

EXERCISE 65.1 | Using Gerunds

Change the sentence to a new sentence beginning with *He remembers*... Add a possessive pronoun if the subject of the gerund is not the same as the subject of *remembers*.

1. He came.   He remembers coming.
2. We came.   He remembers our coming.
3. His sister left.   He remembers her leaving.
4. He learned to drive.   He remembers learning to drive.
5. I asked.   ....
6. They taught him to swim.   ....
7. He took his first trip.   ....
8. His father gave him a penny.   ....
9. He ran away from home.   ....
10. His sister gave him a haircut.   ....
11. His teacher kept him after school. ....
12. He lost all his money.   ....
13. We gave him a bicycle.   ....
14. He played in the park.   ....
15. They took him to the farm.   ....
16. He earned his first dollar.   ....
17. We took him to his first movie.   ....
18. She taught him to dance.   ....
19. He fought with his brother.   ....
20. I took his picture.   ....

EXERCISE 65.2 | Practice with Verbs Followed by Gerund with Subject

Speaker A: Form a question based on the picture.
Speaker B: Respond in terms of the picture using the structure verb + gerund with subject. Study the model.

1.

SPEAKER A: What is Mary worried about?
SPEAKER B: She's worried about her sister Helen's eating so much.

2.

3.

4.

5.

6.

EXERCISE 67.1 | Forming Sentences with NP (Object) + NP or Adj (Complement)

Form good sentences using words or phrases from all four columns. You may change verb tenses and add modifiers.

Example: Everyone / considered / the idea / very dangerous.

Everyone	thought	it	president
I	consider	him	prudent
The students	don't like	the theory	dangerous
We	elect	the idea	quiet
All the students	prove	the explanation	amusing
The doctor	appoint	us	their leader
They	feel	the teachers	confused
He	name	Mrs. Prince	a failure
The teachers	keep	her	wrong
The club	call	them	confusing
No one	imagine	Dr. Wilson	their friends
			"Shorty"
			pleasant
			strangers
			a success
			frightening

EXERCISE 68.1 | Forming Questions Using *or* + Infinitive with Subject

A. Form several questions to ask other members of the class. Use all three columns and begin each question with *Is it*...?

Example: Is it useful / for most people / to speak more than one language?

unusual	old people	speak more than one language
necessary	all doctors	sleep eight hours a night
useful	engineers	have several years' training
easy	language students	live alone
important	most people	know grammar and vocabulary
all right	everyone	know botany
quite hard	young people	tell the truth
unnecessary	children	have leisure time
hard	some people	play all the time
imperative	farmers	get up early

Form two or three questions of your own invention using the same pattern.

EXERCISE 68.2| Summary Exercise: Verb + Gerund/Infinitive/Base Form with Subject

Repeat the original sentence and substitute the cued verbs and adjectives. Make other necessary changes in the complement. Study the three examples.

1. asked — I asked Jean to call.
2. resented — I resented Jean's calling.
3. was anxious — I was anxious for Jean to call.
4. disliked — ....
5. advised — ....
6. told — ....
7. made — ....
8. felt eager — ....
9. was tired of — ....
10. enjoyed — ....
11. looked forward to — ....
12. let — ....
13. expected — ....
14. was afraid — ....
15. forgot about — ....
16. watched — ....
17. recommended — ....
18. was delighted — ....
19. waited — ....
20. laughed about — ....

EXERCISE 68.3| Summary Exercise: Verb + Gerund/Infinitive/Base Form with Subject

Fill the blanks with either the *base form*, the *infinitive* or *gerund* of the verb in parentheses.

(come) 1. I told him .... tomorrow.
(apply) 2. He said he'd like me .... for the job.
(shut) 3. The teacher had me .... the door.
(make) 4. Mother helped Susan .... a costume for the dance.
(come) 5. Mr. and Mrs. Brown are excited about their daughter and her family .... to visit them.
(tell) 6. It wasn't easy for him .... us that.
(join) 7. Let me persuade Bob .... us.
(get) 8. They're happy about their daughter .... married.

(disappear) 9. Using some form of magic, the man made the girl ....
(stop) 10. We told the children .... swimming in that deep lake.
(help) 11. Why don't you ask her .... you?
(play) 12. She worries about the children .... in the street.
(make) 13. Susan always helps her mother .... the bed.
(leave) 14. John's parents didn't recommend his .... school to get a job.
(write) 15. Miss Flower always makes her class .... a long composition every week.

SUMMARY UNIT

This grammar book has dealt with several aspects of the English noun phrase and verb phrase (or predicate).

NOUN PHRASES

Types of structures which occur as noun phrases may include the following.

Mass Noun: *Rice* is the principal food of East Asia.
Count Noun: *Bananas* grow in warm climates.
Noun modified by
    a noun determiner: *The trip* was expensive.
    an adjective: *Hot soup* is delicious.
    a premodifying noun: *Chicken soup* costs sixty cents.
    a prepositional phrase: *People in Quebec* speak French.
    an infinitive: *Some letters to answer* came in the mail.
    a participle: *Frozen icicles* are like *shining knives*.
    a number + noun: *Four-door cars* cost a little more.
Proper noun: *David* had a friend in the government.
Pronoun: *We* can leave our coats here.
Indefinite pronoun: *Everyone* liked Mr. Walker's lecture.
Indefinite pronoun modified by
    an adjective: *Something strange* happened.
    a prepositional phrase: *Someone in Rome* sent it.
Noun substitute: *Another* will be sent tomorrow.
Gerund: *Boxing* is a dangerous sport.
Infinitive: *To succeed* takes a lot of patience.
The + an adjective: *The strong* could just about reach the river.
Compound noun: *Corn flakes* are *breakfast cereal*.

When a noun has more than one modifier, the modifiers occur in a certain order—first determiners, then adjectives (including participles), then pre-modifying nouns. After the head noun come prepositional phrases and infinitives, and gerunds modified by a prepositional phrase.

PRE-DETERMINER	DETERMINER	POST-DETERMINER AND NUMBER	DESCRIPTIVE AND PARTICIPLE	SIZE AND AGE	COLOR	ORIGIN	PRE-MODIFYING NOUN	MODIFIED NOUN
All	every	other	pretty	little	red	Samoan	paper	
some of	the	six	burning	new	beige	northern	bottom	

Two or more noun phrases can be joined by a conjunction, *and* and *or* (or a correlative: *both...and, either...or, neither...nor*) into a compound noun phrase.

John and his father went to the baseball game.
Either the red shed or the white one will fit there.

The types of noun phrase structures described above can be used in these several ways in a sentence (except that pronouns cannot be appositives).

Subject of a verb: *The other five burning houses* collapsed.
Direct object of a verb: She bought *both of the little coral bracelets*.
Indirect object of a verb: She bought *Henry* a bag of candy.
Object of a preposition: I put the slippers in *my bedroom closet*.
Appositive: Mr. Jones, *a tax lawyer,* had a different idea.
Complement of *BE* or a linking verb: Paul is *a chemist*.
Complement of a direct object: I consider him *an expert*.

SENTENCE PATTERNS

In the Introductory Unit a few basic sentence patterns were mentioned—patterns with *BE*, a linking verb, an intransitive verb and a transitive verb. Several more types of sentences have been practiced in this grammar book. In all of them the verb precedes its object or complement; English sentence order is *subject + verb + object* in statement sentences.

TYPE 1   Subject + *BE* or Linking Verb + Complement
      a. Susan was the winner. (complement = a noun phrase)
         Joe became a well-known doctor.
      b. Jackson wasn't happy. (complement = an adjective)
         This answer doesn't seem right.
      c. My radio isn't there. (complement = a place adverb)

TYPE 2	Subject + Transitive Verb + Direct Object (DO)
	a. Children often break their toys. (object = a noun phrase)
	b. Bruce hopes Betty will be there. (object = a sentence)
TYPE 3	Subject + Intransitive Verb
	My car wouldn't start.
TYPE 4	Subject + Verb + Indirect Object (IO) + Direct Object (DO)
	a. This will save you a lot of money. (IO before DO)
	b. George will take some to Mr. Reed. (DO before *to/for* IO)
	c. He wrote to me that he was coming. (*to* IO before sentence DO)
TYPE 5	Subject + Verb + Direct Object + Object Complement
	a. I'd call William an expert. (complement = a noun phrase)
	b. We thought the pilot crazy. (complement = an adjective)
TYPE 6	Subject + Verb + Infinitive
	a. Faye is ready to go to Texas. (verb *BE* + an adjective)
	b. Faye wants to leave tomorrow. (verb = a transitive verb)
TYPE 7	Subject + Verb + Infinitive with Subject
	a. We're ready for Sampson to begin. (verb *BE* + an infinitive)
	b. I'd like (for) us to start early. (verb = a transitive verb)
TYPE 8	Subject + Verb + Base Form with Subject
	He made us repeat the exercise.
TYPE 9	Subject + Verb + Gerund
	Doris enjoys going to the farm.
TYPE 10	Subject + Verb + Gerund with Subject
	a. Everyone worries about Joe's smoking. (gerund subject is possessive)
	b. Nancy remembers him mailing the card. (gerund subject is objective)
TYPE 11	Subject *It* + *BE* + Complement + Infinitive
	a. It's not easy to learn all of it. (complement = an adjective)
	b. It was a shame to miss the party. (complement = a noun phrase)
TYPE 12	Empty Subject *There* + Verb + Real Subject + Complement
	a. There's a squirrel on the roof. *(BE)*
	b. There fell a rock from the sky. (intransitive verb)

INDIRECT SPEECH

Speech which is being reported either directly or indirectly can be thought of as an instance of a complete sentence pattern being used in the role of object of a verb.

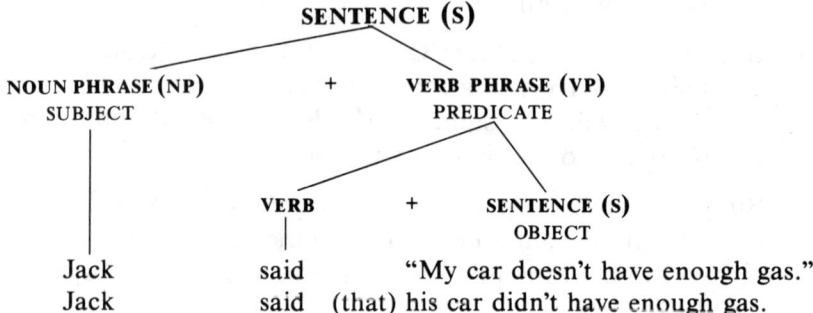

Jack	said	"My car doesn't have enough gas."
Jack	said	(that) his car didn't have enough gas.

In the case of direct speech the reporting verb may be either before or after the quoted material or it may interrupt the quote. In the latter two cases the reporting verb may precede the reporter.

>Jack said, "Mr. Newton raises chickens."
>"Mr. Newton," Jack said, "raises chickens."
>   said Jack,
>"Mr. Newton raises chickens," Jack said.
>   said Jack.

For indirect speech the reporter and the reporting verb must be at the beginning of the sentence. Reported indirect sentences use *that* as a subordinator (optionally); indirect Yes/No questions use *if* or *whether;* indirect *Wh*-questions use the question word in a dual role as subordinator and question word.

When the reporting verb is in the past tense, the tense of the verb of the reported material is usually also changed to past. However, if the statement is still true at the time of reporting, it does not need to be changed to past.

>Carlos asked, "Is Neil Armstrong going to the moon?" (1968)
>Carlos asked if Neil Armstrong was going to the moon. (1970)

>Carlos asked, "Is Miami in Florida?"
>Carlos asked if Miami was (or is) in Florida.

Imperatives are reported in indirect speech as infinitives with subject. There is no subordinator or tense change.

>"Don't get that mud on my rug," said Gloria.
>Gloria said not to get that mud on her rug.

APPENDIX

I. ENGLISH NOUN PLURALS

A. The Regular Plural Suffix

/iz/ after a sibilant or affricate sound:

/s/ bus-busses, box-boxes   /š/ dish-dishes   /č/ watch-watches

/z/ rose-roses   /ž/ loge-loges   /j/ edge-edges

/s/ after a voiceless sound which is not a sibilant or affricate:

/p/ map-maps   /t/ cat-cats   /k/ duck-ducks

/f/ cuff-cuffs, graph-graphs, laugh-laughs   /θ/ month-months

/z/ after a voiced sound which is not a sibilant or affricate:

/b/ robe-robes   /d/ bed-beds   /g/ egg-eggs

/m/ time-times   /n/ son-sons   /ŋ/ wing-wings

/v/ stove-stoves   /ð/ lathe-lathes   /w/ toe-toes, cow-cows

/l/ bell-bells   /r/ door-doors   /y/ tie-ties, day-days

/ɔ/ law-laws   /a/ rah-rahs   /ə/ sofa-sofas

B. Change (Voicing) of Base Before the Regular Suffix

/f/ changes to /v/ —spelled *ve*. (The change is optional for words in parentheses.)

calf-calves, (dwarf-dwarves), elf-elves, half-halves, (hoof, hooves), knife-knives, leaf-leaves, life-lives, loaf-loaves, (scarf-scarves), self-selves, sheaf-sheaves, shelf-shelves, thief-thieves, (wharf-wharves), wife-wives, wolf-wolves

/θ/ changes to /ð/. (The change is optional for all of these. There is no spelling change.)

bath-baths, booth-booths, mouth-mouths, oath-oaths, path-paths, sheath-sheaths, truth-truths, wreath-wreaths, youth-youths

/s/ changes to /z/. (There is no spelling change.)

house-houses

C. The *-en* Suffix

(Two of these have a change in the base as well.)

ox-oxen, child-children, brother (meaning "fellow member")-brethren

D. **No Suffix**

These words change the vowel in the base:

foot-feet, tooth-teeth, goose-geese, louse-lice, mouse-mice, man-men, woman-women

These words have no vowel change: (Many have alternate regular plurals in certain usages.)

aircraft, series, species
deer, fish, grouse, sheep, (and many other game animals)
brace, gross, head, yoke (and some other quantitative and partitive words)
Swiss, Sioux, -*ese nationalities* (and many other tribal and national names)
haiku, sen (and many other words from foreign languages which have no plural)

E. **Foreign Plural Suffixes and Ending Changes**

(The words in parentheses mainly use the foreign plural in technical literature and use the regular plural otherwise.)

Ending -*us* changes to -*i* /ay/.

alumnus-alumni, bacillus-baccilli, (cactus-cacti), fungus-fungi, (nucleus-nuclei), stimulus-stimuli

Ending -*us* changes to -*era* or -*ora* /ɔrə/.

corpus-corpora, genus-genera

Ending -*a* changes to -*ae* /iy/. (the pronunciation of -*ae* varies sometimes)

(antenna-antennae), alga-algae, alumna-alumnae, (formula-formulae), larva-larvae, (nebula-nebulae), (vertebra-vertebrae)

Ending -*um* changes to -*a* /ə/.

addendum-addenda, bacterium-bacteria, erratum-errata, (medium-media), (memorandum-memoranda), ovum-ova, stratum-strata

Endings -*ex* and -*ix* change to -*ices* /isiyz/.

(apex-apices), (appendix-appendices), codex-codices, (index-indices), (latex-latices), (matrix-matrices), (vortex-vortices)

Ending -*nx* changes to -*nges* /njiyz/.

    larynx-larynges, (pharynx-pharynges), (phalanx-phalanges)

Ending -*is* changes to -*es* /iyz/.

    analysis-analyses, axis-axises, basis-bases, crisis-crises, diagnosis-diagnoses, ellipsis-ellipses, hypothesis-hypotheses, oasis-oases, parenthesis-parentheses, synopsis-synopses, thesis-theses

Ending -*on* changes to -*a* /ə/.

    criterion-criteria, phenomenon-phenomena

Ending -*o* changes to -*i* /iy/.

    (libretto-libretti), (virtuoso-virtuosi)

Suffix -*im* /iym/.

    (cherub-cherubim), kibbutz-kibbutzim, (seraph-seraphim)

No change in spelling but the regular English plural suffix is pronounced.

    chamois-chamois, chasis-chassis, corps-corps, faux pas-faux pas
    /šæmiy-šæmiyz/ /čæsiy-čæsiyz/ /kɔr-kɔrz/ /fowpa-fowpaz/

II. USE OF THE ARTICLE *THE* WITH GEOGRAPHICAL NAMES

(Strong stress usually falls on the last word of a name; exceptions are marked.)

A. Names of Natural Geographical Places

	NO **THE** NO GENERIC WORD	NO **THE** WITH GENERIC WORD	NO **THE** GENERIC WORD IS FIRST
Continents	Asia		
Islands	Greenland	Norfolk Island	
Waterfalls		Niagara Falls	
Some bays		Hudson Bay	
Lakes		Crater Lake	Lake Baykal
Points		Montauk Point	Point Barrow
Mountains			Mt. Everest
Most capes			Cape Horn

	ARTICLE **THE** NO GENERIC WORD	ARTICLE **THE** WITH GENERIC WORD	ARTICLE **THE** GENERIC WORD BEFORE **OF**
Mountain ranges	the Alps	the Andes Mountains	
Island groups	the Philippines	the Philippine Islands	
Oceans		the Pacific Ocean	
Seas		the Red Sea	
Channels		the English Channel	
Currents		the Japan Current	
Rivers		the Nile River	
Peninsulas		the Yucatan Peninsula	
Passes		the Khyber Pass	
Valleys		the Rhine Valley	
Deserts		the Sahara Desert	
Canyons		the Grand Canyon	
Gulfs		the Arabian Gulf	the Gulf of Okhotsk
Plateaus		the Colorado Plateau	the Plateau of Tibet
Isthmuses		the Kra Isthmus	the Isthmus of Suez
Some capes			the Cape of Good Hope
Most bays			the Bay of Biscay
Straits			the Strait of Gibraltar

B. Names of Man-made Geographical Places

	NO **THE** NO GENERIC WORD	NO **THE** WITH GENERIC WORD	NO **THE** GENERIC WORD IS FIRST
Countries	Argentina		
States, Provinces	Florida		
Cities, Towns	Bangkok	Mexico City	
U.S. Counties		Orange County	
City streets		Downing St.	
Roads		Columbia Rd.	
Avenues		Fifth Ave.	
Lanes		Maiden Ln.	
Drives		Elizabeth Dr.	
Boulevards		MacArthur Blvd.	
City parks		Ueno Park	
Squares		Trafalgar Square	
Circles		Columbus Circle	
Stations		Victoria Station	
Airports		Dulles Airport	
Stadiums		Yankee Stadium	
Abbeys		Westminster Abbey	
Cathedrals		St. Peter's Cathedral	
Palaces		Buckingham Palace	
Halls		Independence Hall	
Hospitals		Holy Cross Hospital	
Cemeteries		Arlington Cemetery	
Dams		Nurek Dam	
Schools		Ramsey High School	
Colleges		Vassar College	
Universities		Oxford University	
Numbered highway routes			Route 66
Jewish temples			Temple Shalom

	ARTICLE **THE** NO GENERIC WORD	ARTICLE **THE** WITH GENERIC WORD	ARTICLE **THE** GENERIC WORD BEFORE **OF**
Countries	the Netherlands		
Regions	the Levant		
Buildings	the Taj Mahal	the Sears Building	
Houses		the White House	
Rooms		the Rose Room	
Libraries		the Vatican Library	
Theaters	the Globe Theater		
Museums		the British Museum	the Boston Museum of Fine Art
Galleries		the Tate Gallery	the Freer Gallery of Art
Temples		the Todaiji Temple	the Temple of Zeus
Monuments		the Washington Monument	
Memorials		the Lincoln Memorial	
Towers		the Eiffel Tower	the Tower of Babel
Arts Centers		the Kennedy Center	
Institutions		the Smithsonian Institution	
Universities			the University of California
Intercity roads		the Burma Road	
Highways		the Alcan Highway	
Turnpikes		the Pennsylvania Turnpike	
Trails		the Santa Fe Trail	
Tunnels		the Simplon Tunnel	
Bridges		the Golden Gate Bridge	
Canals		the Panama Canal	
Zoos		the Bronx Zoo	

III. MEASURES, CONTAINERS & UNITS FOR FOODS & HOUSEHOLD COMMODITIES

A. Measures

WEIGHT	METRIC EQUIVALENT
ounce (oz.)	
pound (lb.) [= 16 oz.]	1 pound = 454 grams
ton [= 2000 lbs.]	

LIQUID VOLUME	METRIC EQUIVALENT
ounce (oz.)	
pint (pt.) [= 16 oz.]	1 fluid pint = .95 liter
quart (qt.) [2 pts; 32 oz.]	
gallon (gal.) [= 4 qts; 64 oz.]	

DRY VOLUME	METRIC EQUIVALENT
pint (pt.)	1 pint = 1.1 liters
quart (qt.) [= 2 pts.]	
bushel [= 32 qts.]	

B. Containers

bag
(or *sack*): candy, nuts, onions, potatoes, potato chips, rice, flour

basket: peaches, apples, berries, cherries

bottle: soda (pop), wine, soy sauce, catsup, salad dressing, fruit juice

box: doughnuts (usually 12), raisins, cereal, cookies, soap, noodles

can: beans, fruits, vegetables, spices, juice, beer, nuts, sardines, soup, coffee

carton: eggs, cigarettes, milk, ice cream

cup
(or *tub*): yogurt, whipped butter, ice cream

jar: jelly, peanut butter, mayonnaise, pickles, jam

jug: cooking oil, vinegar, cider, milk, bleach

pack: cigarettes (usually 20)

package: cookies, flour, sugar, chewing gum, cheese, butter, napkins

tube: toothpaste

C. Units and Parts

bar:	candy, soap
cube:	butter (usually ¼ lb.)
ear:	corn
head:	lettuce, cabbage, cauliflower
loaf:	bread (usually 1 lb.)
stalk:	celery, rhubarb
stick:	chewing gum, butter
roll:	film, candy, paper towels, wrapping paper
wedge:	cheese
piece:	cheese, bread, pie, cake, lettuce, parsley, celery
pat:	butter (enough for a slice of bread)
slice:	bread, meat, cheese, ice cream
scoop:	ice cream

D. Aggregates

bunch:	carrots, celery, beets, asparagus, parsley, spring onions
six-pack:	soda (pop), beer (a carton of six cans or bottles)
pad (or *tablet*):	writing paper

IV. VERBS AND ADJECTIVES HAVING SPECIAL COMPLEMENTS

VERBS FOLLOWED BY INFINITIVE

SUBJECT	VERB	INFINITIVE	
John	wanted	to stay	home.
He	seems	to have	a cold.

agree	choose	guarantee	mean	seem
appear	decide	happen	need	tend
arrange	desire	have	plan	threaten
ask	expect	hope	promise	used
beg	fail	learn	refuse	want
(not) care	get	manage	request	wish

ADJECTIVES FOLLOWED BY INFINITIVE

SUBJECT	BE	ADJECTIVE	INFINITIVE	
Edna	was	anxious	to go.	
She	isn't	sure	to win	this game.

(un)able	difficult*	interested	smart*
(un)accustomed	disappointed	(un)kind*	sorry
afraid	disturbed	(un)likely*	stupid*
amazed	eager	(un)lucky*	strange*
annoyed	easy*	nice*	supposed
apt	(in)eligible	(dis)pleased	sure
(un)ashamed	expected*	(im)polite*	surprised
bad*	foolish*	(im)possible*	sweet*
bound	free	(un)prepared	terrible*
brave*	fun*	(un)qualified	upset
careful	glad	quick	welcome
careless*	good*	ready	(un)willing
certain	(un)happy	reluctant	(un)wise*
clever*	hard*	sad*	wonderful*
(in)competent	(dis)inclined	satisfied	worried
delighted	impatient	slow	wrong*

*These adjectives also occur in the pattern with the subject *it:* "It was wrong of (or for) her to take everything."

VERBS FOLLOWED BY GERUND

SUBJECT	VERB	GERUND	
They all	enjoyed	going	there.

admit	delay	imagine	postpone	report
advise	deny	include	protest	resent
appreciate	discuss	keep	practice	risk
avoid	dislike	mention	recall	save
confess	enjoy	mind	recommend	stop
consider	escape	miss	relate	suggest
debate	finish	picture	remember	welcome

VERBS FOLLOWED BY INFINITIVE OR GERUND

SUBJECT	AUX.	VERB	INFINITIVE OR GERUND	
Harry	doesn't	like	to walk	in the rain.
Harry	doesn't	like	walking	in the rain.

(can) afford	dread	regret
attempt	forget*	remember*
begin	hate	start
bother	intend	stop*
continue	like	try*
deserve	prefer	

*These verbs have different meanings of the infinitive and the gerund.

VERBS FOLLOWED BY INFINITIVE WITH SUBJECT

SUBJECT OF SENTENCE	VERB	SUBJECT OF INFINITIVE	INFINITIVE	
Mrs. White	asked	Ellie	to stir	the soup.
They	ordered	us	to begin.	

advise	convince	hate	oblige	send
allow	dare	help	order	stimulate
appoint	desire	hire	pay	teach
ask	direct	inspire	permit	telephone
assign	drive	instruct	persuade	tell
assist	elect	intend	phone	tempt
authorize	employ	invite	pick	train
beg	enable	lead	prefer	trust
call	encourage	like	prepare	urge
cause	engage	love	push	want
challenge	expect	meant	raise	warn
choose	forbid	name	remind	wire
command	force	need	request	wish
contract	get	notify	select	write

VERBS FOLLOWED BY GERUND WITH SUBJECT

SUBJECT OF SENTENCE	VERB	SUBJECT OF GERUND	GERUND	
I	appreciate	you/your	telling	me.

admit	denounce	hate	postpone	report
advise	deny	imagine	prefer	resent
announce	disapprove	include	propose	risk
applaud	dislike	like	protest	save
appreciate	dispute	mention	recall	stop
approve	dread	mind	recommend	suggest
concede	end	miss	regret	understand
consider	enjoy	picture	remember	welcome
debate	forget			

VERB AND PREPOSITION FOLLOWED BY GERUND (WITH SUBJECT)

SUBJECT	VERB + PREPOSITION	SUBJECT	GERUND
Mrs. Todd	asked about	Bill's	going.
Mrs. Todd	asked about		going.

admit to	decide against	hear about/of	settle on
agree on/upon	decide on	inquire about	speak about/of
approve of	depend on	insist on	start with
argue about	dream about/of	laugh about	succeed in*
argue against	end with	lie about	talk about/of
ask about	feel like*	look forward to	tell about/of
balk at	fight about	object to	think about/of
begin with	figure on	pay for	warn against/about
believe in	finish with	plan on	wonder about
care about	forget about	refer to	work at*
count on	get around to*	rely on/upon	worry about
cry about	get out of*		

*After these verbs the gerund must not have a subject.

ADJECTIVE AND PREPOSITION FOLLOWED BY GERUND (WITH SUBJECT)

SUBJECT	BE	ADJECTIVE + PREPOSITION	SUBJECT	GERUND
We	were	tired of		standing.
We	were	tired of	his	complaining.

(un)accustomed to	disappointed at/about/over	proud of
afraid of	(un)disturbed about/over	quick at/about*
amazed at	excited about	resigned to
annoyed about/at/with	famous for*	sad about
anxious about	fast at*	(dis)satisfied with
(un)ashamed of	fond of	set on/upon
(un)aware of	glad about	sick of
bad at*	(no) good at*	slow at/about*
bored with	good about	sold on/upon
(in)capable of*	(un)happy about	sorry about
careful about	(un)impressed with	(un)successful in*
careless about	inclined toward	sure of
(un)certain of	interested in	surprised at/about
clever at*	(un)lucky at*	tired of
confident of	new at*	upset about/over
(un)concerned about	opposed to	used to
conscious of	particular about*	worried about
delighted about/with	(dis)pleased with/at	

*After these adjectives the gerund must not have a subject.

VERBS FOLLOWED BY TWO OBJECTS: 1ST FORM—INDIRECT OBJECT AND DIRECT OBJECT
                                2ND FORM—DIRECT OBJECT AND *to* + INDIRECT OBJECT

SUBJECT	AUX.	VERB	I.O.	D.O.	'to' + I.O.
I	'll	send	Alex	a letter.	
I	'll	send		a letter	to Alex.

allow	hand	pay	sell	take
bring	issue	play	send	teach
deliver	lend	present	serve	tell
deny	loan	quote	ship	throw
feed	mail	read	show	trade
furnish	offer	relay	sing	type
give	owe	rent	supply	write
grant	pass			

VERBS FOLLOWED BY TWO OBJECTS: 1ST FORM—INDIRECT OBJECT AND DIRECT OBJECT
                                2ND FORM—DIRECT OBJECT AND *for* + INDIRECT OBJECT

SUBJECT	AUX.	VERB	I.O.	D.O.	'for' + I.O.
The mailman	didn't	leave	us	anything.	
The mailman	didn't	leave		anything	for us.

bake	cook	find	open	reserve
boil	correct	fry	order	save
build	cut	gather	pack	sew
butter	design	get	paint	spin
buy	dial	knit	peel	translate
call	dig	leave	play	wash
catch	do	light	pour	weave
choose	draw	make	prepare	win
construct	earn	mix	print	

VERBS FOLLOWED BY DIRECT OBJECT AND *to* OR *for* + INDIRECT OBJECT (FIXED ORDER)

SUBJECT	AUX.	VERB	D.O.	'to/for' + I.O.
He		introduced	John	to the captain.
I	'll	repeat	the word	for you.

TO	FOR	
explain	answer	open
introduce	cash	pronounce
remember	close	repeat
report	confirm	sign
say	fix	translate
speak	keep	

V. PARTICIPLES USED AS TRUE ADJECTIVES

PRESENT PARTICIPLES

accusing	captivating	demanding	entertaining
adoring	changing	depressing	entrancing
aggravating	charming	disappointing	exasperating
alarming	chastening	disconcerting	exciting
amusing	cheering	discriminating	fascinating
annoying	comforting	disgusting	fitting
appealing	compelling	disparaging	flattering
assuring	condescending	distressing	forbearing
astonishing	confusing	disturbing	forbidding
becoming	consoling	diverting	frightening
believing	convincing	embarrassing	gratifying
bewildering	crushing	enchanting	harassing
biting	daring	encouraging	heartening
boring	dazzling	engaging	horrifying
humiliating	nauseating	repelling	tempting
imposing	obliging	restricting	testing
inspiring	overwhelming	revolting	thrilling
interesting	penetrating	satisfying	threatening
intoxicating	piercing	searching	tiring
intriguing	pleasing	shocking	tormenting

invigorating
inviting
irritating
lasting
menacing
mocking
moving

promising
provoking
punishing
puzzling
reassuring
refreshing
relaxing

sickening
startling
stimulating
stirring
striking
stunning
surprising

troubling
trusting
understanding
upsetting
vexing
willing
winning

PAST PARTICIPLES

admired
agitated
agonized
alarmed
alienated
amused
annoyed
appreciated
aroused
ashamed
assured
astonished
balanced
bewildered
bored
celebrated
charmed
cherished
complicated
confused
contaminated
contented

corrupted
crabbed
debased
degraded
delighted
demoralized
depraved
depressed
deserted
devoted
dignified
disappointed
disgusted
distinguished
disturbed
elated
elevated
embarrassed
enchanted
exasperated
excited
frightened

gratified
guarded
harassed
heartened
heated
honored
horrified
humiliated
hurt
inspired
interested
intoxicated
isolated
noted
obliged
pained
perverted
pleased
qualified
relaxed
resigned
restricted

satisfied
scared
secluded
shaken
shocked
startled
strained
surprised
swollen
terrified
thrilled
tired
troubled
trusted
upset
venerated
unnerved
warped
worried

INDEX

This index gives the number of the *grammatical point* under which the various topics are found.

A little, a few, a lot of, lots of
    As Determiner [11]
    As Substitute [12]

Adjectives [4, 14, 17, 21, 22, 37, 38, 48, 51, 57, 67]

Adverbials (of Time and Place) [34]

Adverbs
    Very Intensifier [11]
    Time and Place [34]

All [19, 20]

Another/other [16, 20]

Appositives [52]

Articles [6] (See also Determiners)

Base Form of Verb [64]

BE (in Special Verb Expressions) [36]

Both [19, 20]

Bring/take [34]

But [49]

Capitalization
    Proper Nouns [1]
    Direct Speech [25]

Collective Nouns [50]

Come/go [34]

Complements [43, 66, 67]

Compound Noun Phrases [47]

Compound Nouns [46, 56]

Conjunctions [47, 48, 49]

Count Nouns [2, 3]

Demonstratives
    As Determiner [6]
    As Substitute [12]

Determiners [5, 6, 10, 11, 15, 16, 19, 20]

Direct Objects (and Indirect Objects) [24, 26, 60, 61, 62]

Direct Speech [25]

Each/every [16, 19, 20]

Either/neither [16, 20]

Else [17]

Enough
    As Determiner [10]
    As Substitute [12]

For (Preposition) [61, 68]

Gerund [40, 41, 42, 43, 44, 53, 65]

If/whether (in Direct Speech) [31]

Imperative [32]

Indefinite Pronouns [17]

Indirect Objects (and Direct Objects) [26, 60, 61, 62]

Indirect Questions [30, 31]

Indirect Speech [26, 27, 30, 31, 32, 33, 34]

Infinitives [32, 35, 36, 37, 38, 39, 42, 43, 44, 53, 55, 63]

Intransitive Verbs (*-ing* Forms as Modifiers) [56]

It (as Sentence Subject) [44]

Many/much
    As Determiner [11, 12]
    As Substitute [20]

Mass Nouns [2, 3]

Modals in Indirect Speech [27]

Modifiers (See Noun Modifiers, Prepositional Phrases)

More/most
    As Determiner [10]
    As Intensifier [57]

Negation [6, 11, 12, 32, 43, 63]

No (as Determiner) [6]

Nominal Phrase [45, 46]

Nominals (Adjectives Used as) [51]

None (as Substitute) [12]

Nouns (See Count Nouns, Mass Nouns)

Noun Compounds [46, 56]

Noun Determiners (See Determiners)

Noun Modifiers [4, 7, 8, 23, 45, 54, 55, 56, 58]

Noun Phrases [1, 7, 13, 18, 22, 47, 51]
(See also Nominal Phrase)

Noun Substitutes [12, 16]
    Question Words as Substitutes [29, 41]

Number Agreement [50, 51]

Numbers [20, 54]

Object Complements [66, 67]

Object Pronouns [9, 63, 64, 65, 68]

Objects (See Direct Objects, Indirect Objects)

One (as Substitute) [12, 16, 20, 21, 45]

Order
    Of Adjectives [14, 23]
    Of Determiners [20]
    Of Nouns [50]

Other/another [16, 20]

Participles (as Noun Modifiers) [56, 58, 59]

Past Perfect Tense (in Indirect Speech) [27]

Plenty of [10]

Plural
    Form of Nouns [1]
    Special Nouns [50]

Possessives [4, 12]

Personal Pronouns [9, 19, 33]

Predeterminers [20]

Preposition + Gerund [41]

Prepositional Phrases (as Modifier) [8, 17, 56, 58]

Pronouns (See Personal Pronouns, Object Pronouns)

Proper Nouns [1]

Punctuation [25]

Purpose (with Infinitive) [39]

Question Words [29, 30]

Reported Speech (See Indirect Speech)

Say/tell [26]

Sentences (as Objects) [24]

Short Answers [38]

Some/any
    As Determiner [5, 15]
    As Substitute [12]
    As Predeterminer [20]

Special Verb Expressions [36]

Stress and Intonation [15, 45, 46, 52, 56]

Subjects [43, 44]

Subordinators [24, 31]

Tenses (in Indirect Speech) [27, 28]

That
    As Subordinator [24, 26]
    Substitute for Gerund and Infinitive [41]

The [6, 51]

There (as Sentence Subject) [44]

To (Preposition) [60]

Transitive Verbs [24]

Two-word Verbs [41]

Verb + Gerund [40]

Verb + Infinitive [35]

Verb Forms
    In Indirect Speech [27]
    Base Form [64]

Verbal Nouns (Gerunds and Infinitives) [43]

Verbs (See Infinitives, Intransitive Verbs, Transitive Verbs, Two-word Verbs)

Wh-Questions [29, 30]

Which, what, whose (as Determiners) [20]

Yes/No Questions [31]

ANSWER KEY

SECTION 1

(Exercise 2.1)
Plural: 2, 4, 5, 7, 10; The others are mass nouns.

(Exercise 2.2)
A: (1) piece/slice; (2) bunch...head; (3) loaves...loaf...loaf...slice/piece; (4) pair; (5) bowl/cup...glass/bottle; (6) tube; (7) gallons; (8) piece; (9) bunches...heads; (10) bars/pieces; (11) bottle; (12) cup
B: (1) Yes, we have to get four rolls; (2) Yes, we got two bags; (3) Yes, we have two bunches; (4) Yes, please bring a bottle; (5) Yes, it's three tubes for a dollar; (6) Yes, please get a loaf; (7) He picked two baskets of peaches; (8) Yes, please get a head; (9) Yes, I need a dozen more; (10) Yes, he's taking five cans; (11) We have one jar; (12) She eats one cup; (13) Yes, I bought two cartons; (14) Four boxes of cereal; (15) We only had two bottles

(Exercise 3.1)
(1) mass, count; (2) mass, count; (3) count, mass; (4) count, mass; (5) count, mass; (6) count, mass; (7) count, mass; (8) count, mass; (9) mass, count; (10) count, mass

(Exercise 4.1)
B: (1) plaster lions...historic; (2) deep green color...lovely Caribbean; (3) French town...Charlemagne's tomb; (4) excellent oil paint...metal surfaces; (5) church's marble floors; (6) high hills...marvelous overall view; (7) a small collection...emperor's treasurers; (8) interesting papers...Pushkin's poetry; (9) latest mail order catalogue; (10) foreign landowners...big farms

(Exercise 6.1)
(1) a...a; (2) the...the; (3) a...the; (4) a...the; (5) The...the; (6) a...a; (7) A...the; (8) the; (9) The...the; (10) the (*an* is possible if there is more than one appendix in the book)...the

(Exercise 7.1)
(1) Dexter (name), two mistakes (number + count noun); (2) No passengers (determiner + count noun), lawyers (count noun); (3) Bill's wife (noun possessive + count noun), fur coats (premodifying noun + count noun); (4) The Parkers (determiner + name), fresh milk (adjective + mass noun); (5) Grape jelly (premodifying noun + mass noun), sale (count noun); (6) Mr. Fields (name), some stale bread (determiner + adjective + mass noun); (7) The two girls (determiner + number + count noun), the chicken soup (determiner + premodifying noun + mass noun); (8) Betty's baby brother (noun possessive + premodifying noun + count noun), a cold (determiner + count noun)

SECTION 2

(Exercise 9.1)
(1) It...her; (2) One of them/He...one; (3) It...her; (4) us...we; (5) They...him; (6) his...us; (7) our...it; (8) She...their

(Exercise 11.1)
(1) many/lots of/a lot of; (2) much/a great deal of/a lot of; (3) much; (4) a lot of/a great deal of/lots of/a little/a little bit of; (5) a few; (6) a lot of/a great deal of/a little/a little bit of; (7) little; (8) Few

(Exercise 11.2)
a/my...the...many/a lot of/lots of...The/A...the...the...the...some/many/a lot of...some/many...a...some...some...some / a little...the/my...a...the...a/my

(Exercise 12.1)
(1) his; (2) yours; (3) ours; (4) mine; (5) hers; (6) theirs

(Exercise 13.1)
her...my...it; my...his...hers...She's...her; They...theirs...ours; mine...yours; them...us; it

(Exercise 13.2)
(1) a few; (2) Few; (3) A few...a lot; (4) some...any; (5) many...some; (6) enough...more; (7) more...enough; (8) That; (9) that one; (10) that; (11) her...hers; (12) hers; (13) Many...much; (14) a lot of...much

SECTION 3

(Exercise 14.1)
(1) a colorful new; (2) seven big red; (3) those rusty old; (4) Whose new blue; (5) that delicious pink; (6) beautiful new white

(Exercise 14.2)
(1) a beautiful old Dutch; (2) an excellent new English; (3) an interesting old Spanish; (4) some marvelous old French; (5) a famous young Japanese; (6) an interesting new Italian

(Exercise 16.1)
(1) the other (one); (2) another (one); (3) the other (one); (4) others; (5) the others; (6) another (one); (7) the other (one); (8) another (one); (9) the others; (10) others

(Exercise 16.2)
(1) The others couldn't come; (2) May I use the others? (3) The other is too small; (4) There are others in the kitchen; (5) Let's take another; (6) Others were listening; (7) Do you have others? (8) There's another at 2:00; (9) The other doesn't work; (10) Do you have any others that are cheaper?

(Exercise 17.1)
(1) anything; (2) anyone/anybody; (3) No one/Nobody/Someone/Somebody; (4) something/nothing; (5) nobody/no one/someone/somebody; (6) someone/somebody; (7) anything; (8) someone/somebody/no one/nobody/something/nothing

(Exercise 17.2)
(1) Do they eat anything else? (2) Has he written a book about anything else? (3) Has anyone/anybody else stopped buying it? (4) Are they sold in anything else? (5) Did she want to make anything else? (6) Did anyone/anybody else enjoy it? (7) Did you meet anybody/anyone else? (8) Did anyone/anybody else gobble one down quickly?

(Exercise 18.1)
(1) most stores (DET. + COUNT N.), either (N. SUBSTITUTE); (2) several other students (DET. + DET. + COUNT N.), bad colds in the head (ADJ. + COUNT N. + PREP. PHRASE); (3) each one (DET. + N. SUBSTITUTE), something else (INDEFINITE PRONOUN + ADJ.); (4) every door on our block (DET. + COUNT N. + PREP. PHRASE), the same number of windows (DET. + ADJ. + COUNT N. + PREP. PHRASE); (5) anyone you know (INDEFINITE PRONOUN + CLAUSE), these delicious little green pickles (DET. + ADJ. + ADJ. + ADJ. + COUNT N.); (6) I (PRONOUN), the manager (DET. + COUNT N.), the one in the blue coat (DET. + N. SUBSTITUTE + PREP. PHRASE); (7) most (N. SUBSTITUTE), mine (POSSESSIVE PRONOUN), three (NUMBER), John's (N. POSSESSIVE); (8) Anita (NAME), you (PRONOUN), a great deal (N. SUBSTITUTE), citrus fruits (PREMODIFYING N. + COUNT N.)

SECTION 4

(Exercise 19.1)
(1) All plants; (2) Not all grass; (3) All dogs; (4) not all boys; (5) All people; (6) All houses; (7) Not all people; (8) All children; (9) all workers; (10) Not all young children; (11) Not all men; (12) Not all boys

(Exercise 19.2)
(1) a few; (2) a little; (3) any; (4) any; (5) Both; (6) neither; (7) Either; (8) much; (9) a great deal; (10) another; (11) none; (12) a lot of; (13) much; (14) each; (15) anyone; (16) every; (17) All; (18) it; (19) the other; (20) every one

(Exercise 20.1)
These are possible answers: (1) customers; (2) courses; (3) brothers; (4) building materials; (5) children; (6) money; (7) Joe and Joan; (8) animals; (9) boys; (10) child; (11) days

(Exercise 20.3)
(1) much of it; (2) a few of those; (3) many of them; (4) some of them; (5) all of it; (6) either of these; (7) both of them; (8) neither of them; (9) a little of it; (10) every one of them; (12) each one of them

(Exercise 22.1)
(1) fine Irish linen; (2) green Burmese jade bracelets; (3) old pink Italian vases; (4) beautiful new French skirt; (5) long red German sausage; (6) old stone Indian axe; (7) small white Japanese trucks; (8) rich brown Colombian coffee; (9) convenient new downtown office; (10) big new Texas ranch

Grammar Point 23, Page 39: students (COUNT N.), some (N. SUBSTITUTE), country (COUNT N.), John's (POSSESSIVE N.), lady (COUNT N.), anyone (INDEFINITE PRONOUN), engineering student (COUNT N.); Page 40: money (MASS N.), few (N. SUBSTITUTE), something (INDEFINITE PRONOUN), ladies (COUNT N.), one (N. SUBSTITUTE), everything (INDEFINITE PRONOUN), all (N. SUBSTITUTE)

(Exercise 23.2)
a...other...a lot of...a few...the...Many...great many of...the...others; Neither...nor...one...both...all...our; a...a few...the...each...many; a little...another...them...My...either...more...the; another

SECTION 5

(Exercise 24.1)
(1) Mary (NP); (2) that they didn't know (S); (3) she wanted to come with us (S); (4) that little boy in the green sweater (NP); (5) English (NP); (6) a party (NP); (7) I can't do it (S); (8) a marvelous old Dutch painting (NP); (9) him (NP); (10) he'll be able to come (S)

(Exercise 24.2)
(1) No, he said he was taking her to Joe's Diner; (2) No, he said he listened to tapes every chance he gets; (3) No, I said I wanted you to come to the dance; (4) No, he said he wanted to become a famous chef; (5) No, she said she was going to take a vacation then; (6) No, he told me she didn't know about it; (7) No, he told me he rode the bus to work with her; (8) No, she told me it was choking on a bone; (9) No, she told me he dreamed about it quite often; (10) No, he/she told her that he was nibbling it.

(Exercise 25.1)
(1) I said, "I don't know how to dance." (2) "Can you come to my party?" she wanted to know. (3) "We're late," I said, "and we're going to miss the bus." (4) "Where are we going?" I asked. (5) He asked in a low voice, "Who's that girl over there?" (6) "That's Margaret," I answered. (7) "Why can't we come?" the children asked. (8) "I want to tell you something," June said to Anne. (9) "What time are you going," I asked, "and when will you be back?" (10) "How did man learn to write?" the professor asked.

(Exercise 26.1)
(1) say; (2) told; (3) tell; (4) tell; (5) said; (6) told; (7) tell; (8) tell; (9) told; (10) told; (11) said; (12) say; (13) said; (14) said; (15) say

(Exercise 26.2)
(1) Mrs. Wilde said (that) she was fluent in Spanish and French; (2) Mary said (that) she practiced all the time; (3) Mr. Forest said (that) he (had) asked Bill to wash his new car; (4) Helen said (that) Jim wanted to meet her friend June; (5) Tom said (that) he always invited them to his parties; (6) Milly said (that) she was trying to turn off the water in the kitchen; (7) Mrs. Collins said (that) she was going to Canada; (8) Mr. Johnson said (that) someone was waving a white handkerchief; (9) Mike said (that) he didn't like cafeterias; (10) Janet said (that) it was printed in the appendix.

(Exercise 27.1)
(1) I said, "I want to go." (2) Jane said, "I am very anxious to come." (3) Bill said, "I will tell you all about it." (4) Barbara said, "I'm engaged to be married." (5) Mr. Wells said, "I have to stop smoking." (6) Mrs. Forest said, "I can't find my son." (7) I said, "I don't want to miss it for anything." (8) Jackie said, "I might/may study Arabic."

(Exercise 28.1)
(1) ...the cook's still working on my/his order; (2) ...Mrs. Chang owned the restaurant; (3) ...was out for a minute; (4) ...they've sent him to a tropical country; (5) ...he's studying prehistoric pottery; (6) ...she wasn't going to eat that cake.

SECTION 6

(Exercise 29.1)
Change *Who* to *Whom* in 1, 2, 4, 7, 8, 9, 10. No change in 3, 5, 6.

(Exercise 29.2)
(1) When's he leaving? (2) How's... (3) Who'll... (4) How long is... (5) How often does... (6) Why was... (7) How far is... (8) Who's... (9) How long are... (10) How are... (11) Whose book is that? (12) How much is... (13) Who(m) did he meet in Brazil? (14) How wide was... (15) Whose books are those?

(Exercise 30.1)
(1) Tom asked Charles where he lived; (2) Mary asked her mother what she should do; (3) Mr. White asked Mr. Smith when he saw Mr. Black; (4) Bob asked Jim how he met Miss Wu; (5) Helen asked her mother why she had to invite Barbara; (6) Mary asked how Tom could go; (7) Bob asked Jim who that new student was; (8) The teacher asked Dan why he was late; (9) Mr. Jones asked his wife when dinner would be ready; (10) Steve asked Jim why he couldn't go; (11) Mr. Jones asked Bob what languages he spoke; (12) Mary asked Tom when he could go.

(Exercise 30.2)
(1) I don't know who he is; (2) ...whose book it is; (3) ...why he can't go; (4) ...how many languages he speaks; (5) ...what he said; (6) ...when it begins; (7) ...where they are; (8) ...how long they're going to stay; (9) ...what time it starts; (10) ...where she's from.

SECTION 7

(Exercise 31.1)
(1) He wanted to know if/whether they were planning to go; (2) Jim asked Tom if/whether he had to leave; (3) Mary asked if/whether they were engaged; (4) They asked if/whether they could use the container; (5) Mrs. Brown asked me if/whether the cheese was from Denmark; (6) The teacher asked June if/whether she knew the answer; (7) The teacher asked Henry if/whether he solved the problem; (8) Bill asked Helen if/whether Jane told her that; (9) I asked Mary if she could go; (10) I asked Mary's mother if/whether she/Mary could go.

(Exercise 31.2)
A: (2) I asked the bus driver whether he had change for a dollar or not; (3) Dr. Hunter asked me whether I took the/any medicine regularly or not; (4) I asked the druggist whether the drug was dangerous to the heart or not; (5) I asked him whether he knew that Dr. Long was my friend or not.

(Exercise 31.4)
Partial key: (1) I asked if you lived around here; (2) I asked if you were from this area; (3) I asked where your parents were born; (4) I asked if you enjoyed winter sports; (5) I asked what you liked to do on weekends; (6) I asked if you had a favorite movie star; (7) I asked if you wanted to go to a movie with me; (8) I asked if you could type sixty words a minute; (9) I asked if you would like to see my rock collection; (10) I asked if you had a rich uncle.

(Exercise 31.5)
(1) They asked Bill, "Where are you going?" (2) She asked Carlos, "Do you speak English?" (3) Mrs. Long asked her son, "Will you help me?" (4) We asked them, "Will you go with us?" (5) I asked, "Are there many applicants?" (6) He asked her, "Do you really want to go?" (7) He asked, "Who are/were they?" (8) Helen asked her friend, "Do you know Tom?"

(Exercise 32.1)
(2) She told them to be quiet; (3) They told me to come early; (4) She told him not to be late; (5) He told him to get plenty of rest; (6) He told her not to tell anyone; (7) He told him/her not to move; (8) She told them to write the words in their notebooks.

(Exercise 32.2)
(1) I asked Bob if/whether Bill was a good friend of his; (2) Tom asked Henry if/whether he wrote/had written his composition; (3) The policeman told the children not to play in the street; (4) Mrs. Thompson asked me if/whether I had heard the good news; (5) Mrs. Palmer told Barbara she had to hurry; (6) Mr. Fama asked me whose car that was; (7) Bob asked Tom which one he wanted; (8) Mrs. White told Helen not to run in front of the cars; (9) He said a good deal of French was spoken in Canada; (10) Mrs. Brown asked me if/whether I should tell him; (11) Mr. Jones told his son he couldn't go out; (12) I said I saw him last night; (13) Tom asked Henry why he did/had done that; (14) Mr. Brown told Tom to do his homework; (15) They said they might not be able to go; (16) Steve asked his brother where he put his watch.

(Exercise 32.3)
Partial key A: (1) "Sit down, please." (2) "Go to bed now, children." (3) "Don't cry, dear." (or) "Stop crying now." (4) "We're out of gas." (5) "Get the newspaper." (or) "Bring the paper to me." (6) "Which movie do you want to go to?" (7) "Be quiet, please." (8) "Do you have the tickets?" (9) "You can't park here, Mister." (or) "There's no parking here, Sir." (10) "Would you like to eat dinner there?" (or) "Do you like Chinese food?"

SECTION 8

(Exercise 33.1)
B: (2) Mr. White said it was only eleven o'clock; (3) Mr. Brown said their meeting started at eleven fifteen; (4) Mr. White said he had all their papers ready; (5) Mr. Brown said they'd have to hurry.
C: I told Mr. White that we were going to be late; (2) He told me that it was only eleven o'clock; (3) I told him that our meeting started at 11:15; (4) He told me that he had all our papers ready; (5) I told him that we'd have to hurry.

(Exercise 34.1)
(1) the next day; (2) there then; (3) this afternoon; (4) tomorrow; (5) this week; (6) here the week before last; (7) four years ago; (8) yesterday morning; (9) a few hours ago (or) this morning; (10) three months ago (or) last June

(Exercise 34.2)
(1) that...had come; (2) held/holds...there; (3) brought/took you with him; (4) taken you...before; (5) were/are; (6) was...would; (7) you would; (8) would have to take you; (9) couldn't...last night; (10) had to...this morning

SECTION 9

(Exercise 35.1)
(1) Yes, but I didn't promise to take her home. (2) Yes, but I didn't attempt to reduce the gas bill. (3) Yes, but I didn't try to play it. (4) Yes, but she doesn't want to interrupt him. (5) Yes, but she doesn't expect to meet Mr. Collier today. (6) Yes, but he doesn't need to take an umbrella. (7) Yes, but they don't want to use chopsticks. (8) Yes, but I don't wish to order it now.

(Exercise 36.1)
(A)
3. Speaker A: Have they decided to go?
   Speaker B: Yes, they have.
4. Speaker A: Will she be able to help us?
   Speaker B: No, she won't.
5. Speaker A: Does he have to get a haircut?
   Speaker B: Yes, he does.
6. Speaker A: Is he willing to drive?
   Speaker B: No, he isn't.
7. Speaker A: Was she pleased to hear the news?
   Speaker B: Yes, she was.
8. Speaker A: Does Mrs. White expect to be home this afternoon?
   Speaker B: Yes, she does.
9. Speaker A: Has John been able to save any money?
   Speaker B: No, he hasn't.
10. Speaker A: Are they going to take tennis lessons?
    Speaker B: Yes, they are.
11. Speaker A: Will we need to tell them when we're going?
    Speaker B: Yes, we will.

(B) These are the tag endings for the questions of Speaker A, and the expected short answers of Speaker B.
3. Speaker A: ...haven't they?
   Speaker B: Yes, they have.
4. Speaker A: ...will she?
   Speaker B: No, she won't.
5. Speaker A: ...doesn't he?
   Speaker B: Yes, he does.
6. Speaker A: ...is he?
   Speaker B: No, he isn't.
7. Speaker A: ...wasn't she?
   Speaker B: Yes, she was.
8. Speaker A: ...doesn't she?
   Speaker B: Yes, she does.
9. Speaker A: ...has he?
   Speaker B: No, he hasn't.
10. Speaker A: ...aren't they?
    Speaker B: Yes, they are.
11. Speaker A: ...won't we?
    Speaker B: Yes, we will.

(Exercise 37.1)
Any reasonable answer will do.

(Exercise 38.1)
(1) Yes, they're about to. (2) No, she won't be able to. (3) Yes, we're supposed to. (4) Yes, I'm going to. (5) No, I'm not anxious to. (6) Yes, he does. (7) No, they haven't. (8) No, he didn't want to. (9) Yes, they are. (10) Yes, they intend to.

(Exercise 39.1)
Numbers 2, 5 and 7—no change possible; not infinitives of purpose.

(Exercise 39.2)
(2) ...to eat lunch. (3) ...to take a walk. (4) ...to get (to ask for) some information. (5) ...to find the meaning of the word. (6) ...to eat (to have) dinner. (7) ...to get (to buy) some stamps. (8) ...to cure (to relieve, to help) my cold. (9) ...to get the butter. (10) ...to get some much needed rest.

SECTION 10

(Exercise 41.1)
(1) She suggested going downtown to shop. (2) They're looking forward to starting their vacation next Saturday. (3) He's about to finish reading the book. (4) He's good at playing tennis. (5) She's trying to give up smoking. (6) She's excited about going to her first dance. (7) They enjoy listening to stories (or to their grandfather telling them stories) (or to having their grandfather tell them stories) (8) She admitted causing the accident.

(Exercise 42.1)
No change possible in Sentences 1, 2, 3, 6, 8, 9, 11, 13, 14, 15, 16

(Exercise 42.2)
(3) flying; (4) to tell; (5) to do; (6) to return; (7) to thank; (8) thanking; (9) to write/writing; (10) go...going; (11) washing; (12) fixing; (13) to do/doing; (14) to take/taking; (15) to do/doing; (16) to rain/raining; (17) to cook; (18) teaching; (19) losing; (20) to thank; (21) to be; (22) to do; (23) memorizing; (24) buying; (25) go; (26) to have/having; (27) to tell/telling; (28) reading; (29) working; (30) doing

(Exercise 42.3)
There is no one correct answer.

(Exercise 43.1)
(2) Not studying... (3) Preparing food for the party... (4) ...inviting Aunt Ellis for dinner (on) Saturday; (5) ...afraid of driving at night; (6) Listening to tapes... (7) Smoking in this section of the airplane... (8) ...meeting (your) friends in Japan? (9) ...swimming, hiking, playing tennis in the summertime. (10) Talking out loud to yourself... (11) ...making a mistake in a new job; (12) Waiting (long) hours for someone... (13) ...writing his new textbook a few weeks ago. (14) Swimming two hours every day or taking some other kind of exercise... (15) ...walking on the beach, getting out in the sun and smelling the salt air.

(Exercise 44.1)
(1) There were fourteen students in class today. (2) There was a castle on the top of the hill. (3) There was some wine in the bottle. (4) There were two men working on the problem. (5) There were some red flowers in bloom in the garden. (6) There will be a new dress shop opening here soon. (7) There were two boys hiking in the woods. (8) There were several people picnicking by the river.

SECTION 11

(Exercise 45.1)
(1) a large new brick house; (2) an old brown leather coat; (3) a big new steel bridge; (4) another beautiful new silk dress; (5) two interesting little Japanese dolls; (6) two ugly old Boston hotels; (7) that quiet little country retreat; (8) my usual long morning walk; (9) the traditional English Christmas pudding

(Exercise 46.1)
(1) room; (2) one; (3) dwellers; (4) ones; (5) one; (6) utensils; (7) shop; (8) trip; (9) one; (10) glasses

(Exercise 46.2)
(2) A milk carton. (3) On the serving tray. (4) A cream pitcher. (5) Salad oil. (6) In the cookie jar. (7) A flower pot. (8) A window pane. (9) A cookbook. (10) A boxing match. (11) In the play pen. (12) A teddy bear. (13) Wine glasses.

SECTION 12

(Exercise 47.2)

There is no one correct answer. Here is one possible answer among many. (1) Why do you think neither Margaret nor June will tell us what happened? (2) I've heard that he neither drinks nor smokes. (3) Neither Barbara nor Harriet will buy coffee because of the high price in the stores at the present time. (4) Neither Mr. White nor Mr. Smith would tell us what happened in the meeting today. (5) Neither the clothing store nor the department store had the kind of shoes that Jack always buys. (6) The old man pretended that he could neither see nor hear. (7) She said that neither Jim nor Bob would help her with her math lesson. (8) The history course taught by Professor Whitehall was neither interesting nor useful in my opinion. (9) She serves neither bread nor cookies to her family because she feels they are not good for her family.

(Exercise 48.1)

(2) He likes to swim, dance and play tennis. (or) He likes to swim, to dance and to play tennis. (3) You should either come on time or not come at all. (4) He was big and heavy. (5) You must stand up and fight for your principles. (6) She looked the word up in the dictionary and told us how to pronounce it. (7) The building was modern, functional and beautiful.

(Exercise 49.1)

A: (2) He likes history and he likes mathematics. (3) The problem was hard but it wasn't impossible. (4) He was angry, but he was not violent. (5) She was tall and she was very attractive. (6) She likes Charles, but she doesn't like his friends. (7) He works hard all day and he works hard all night. (8) He was tired, but he wasn't very sleepy.
B: (2) He likes history and mathematics. (3) The problem was hard, but not impossible. (4) He was angry, but not violent. (5) She was tall and very attractive. (6) She likes Charles, but not his friends. (7) He works hard all day and night. (8) He was tired, but not very sleepy.

(Exercise 49.2)

There is no one correct answer. One possible completion is given here. (2) Neither the teacher nor the students liked the textbook. (3) He was short and quite fat. (4) I'll see you either this Friday or a week from Friday. (5) I take cream but not sugar. (6) He laughed and said he agreed with me. (7) I got to the bus stop on time but I had forgotten my briefcase and had to return home. (8) We had neither time nor money. (9) Did Tom or Bob invite you to go camping with them? (10) I like both my brother and my sister. (11) I can speak both English and Japanese fluently. (12) John promised to come early and help us.

(Exercise 50.1)

(1) was; (2) were; (3) Was; (4) was; (5) were; (6) was; (7) were; (8) was; (9) were; (10) was

SECTION 13

(Exercise 51.1)

(1) is; (2) are; (3) survive; (4) becomes; (5) is; (6) find; (7) are; (8) is

(Exercise 52.1)

(1) ...Mr. Jones, who is a friend of mine. (2) ...Teheran, which was my home for two years. (3) And Jane, who was my mother's sister,... (4) ...Robert Thomas, who was one of the most famous engineers in the world. (5) ...dacron, which is one of the best synthetic materials. (6) Mr. Long, who is our country's ambassador to Australia, ... (7) Basketball, which is a very fast game, ...

(Exercise 52.3)

(1) These unusual pictures were taken by Henry Long, the famous photographer. (2) Those buildings were designed by Mr. Steel, our architect. (3) An important discovery was made by Dr. Watts, a famous scientist. (4) That book was written by Elizabeth Conrad, a modern novelist. (5) The lecture will be given by Dr. Dale, a professor at the university. (6) Those valuable objects were discovered by Dr. Short, a famous archaeologist.

(Exercise 53.1)

(1) to visit; (2) to mail; (3) writing; (4) promising; (5) to forget; (6) to call...to call; (7) raining; (8) to go...to go; (9) to close (Some speakers say "closing" in this sentence); (10) closing; (11) to invite; (12) taking

(Exercise 54.1)

(1) ...a fifty-pound sack of rice. (2)...a two-hour exam; (3)...a five hundred-page book; (4)...a six-day trip; (5)...a three-bedroom house; (6)...a fifteen-minute movie; (7)...a ten-cent stamp; (8)...a two-hour lecture; (9)...a fifty thousand-dollar house; (10)...a thirty-minute rest

(Exercise 54.2)

There is no one correct answer. One possible answer is given as an example. (1) *a two-page composition*—The teacher asked them to write a two-page composition by tomorrow. (2) *five-dollar tickets*—For his birthday we gave him two five-dollar tickets to the soccer match. (3) *a five-mile walk*—It's a five-mile walk to the post office from where we live. (4) *a six-hour flight*—After we left Costa Rica, we had a six-hour flight to Santiago, Chile. (5) *a two-hour conversation*—I went to her office where we had a pleasant two-hour conversation about the theater. (6) *a fifty-dollar suit*—I think Jack's still wearing that fifty-dollar suit he bought ten years ago.

(Exercise 55.1)

(2) ...phone number to remember. (3) ...a place to spend your vacation. (4) ...fifty dollars to spend on a sewing machine. (5) ...a man to trust. (6) ...exercises to do. (7) ...potato salad to eat. (8) ...a mile back to eat at.

(Exercise 56.1)
(1) A falling tree. (2) A barking dog. (3) Running water. (4) A sleeping bear. (5) Burning leaves. (6) A crying baby.

SECTION 14

(Exercise 57.1)
Very can be used in Sentences 3, 4, 7, 8, 10, 12, 14, 15. There is no one correct answer for the remaining sentences, but we give one possibility. (5) Yes, it was working well. (6) Yes, it's boiling furiously (or hard). (9) Yes, it was blowing hard. (11) Yes, it's ringing loudly. (13) Yes, they're growing fast.

(Exercise 58.1)
Very, rather, quite, etc. can be used in Sentences 1, 4, 6, 7. There is no one correct answer for the remaining sentences. This is one possibility. (2) The man *quietly* hiding in the woods ran when he saw us. (3) We watched the *slowly (rapidly)* disappearing sun. (5) She tried to quiet the *loudly* crying children. (8) They cheered their *recently* elected leader. (13) We took a drive through the *badly* damaged area. (14) I saw a *frequently* repeated program on TV last night. (15) What can we do about *sharply (rapidly)* increasing costs?

(Exercise 58.2)
(1) We took a picture of an interesting old stone bridge built in 1732. (2) We have several very satisfied customers doing business with us. (3) We stayed in a beautiful new five hundred-room hotel located in the center of the city. (4) He works in a large fifty-story office building designed by Mr. Oda, a Japanese architect educated in Sweden.

(Exercise 59.1)
(1) broken; (2) boring; (3) amusing; (4) tiring; (5) frozen; (6) running; (7) tired; (8) convincing; (9) visiting; (10) continuing; (11) missing; (12) rented; (13) closed; (14) worried; (15) accompanying; (16) exciting; (17) spoken; (18) beginning; (19) understanding; (20) following

(Exercise 59.2)
(1) The puzzled little boy didn't know where he was. (2) The little boy, confused by all the noise, began crying for his parents. (3) That woman digging in the garden is becoming red in the face. (4) That little girl holding the flowers is charming. (5) He told us an astonishing story. (6) She put the cooked vegetables on the table. (7) We returned late from our tiring trip. (8) You'd better tell that man chopping the tree to be careful. (9) Where can I take my broken watch to be repaired? (10) The crops planted in that field look dry.

SECTION 15

(Exercise 62.1)
The order cannot be changed in Sentences 2, 4, 5, 6, 9, 11, 13, 14. This is the changed order in the other sentences. (1) ...me some money. (3) ...my friends money. (7) ...my brother some nice cufflinks. (8) ...Mr. Wells his raincoat. (10) ...my sister a purse... (12) ...Charles a letter... (15) ...me his son's picture.

(Exercise 62.2)
(1) Please write him a letter. (2) She bought Mary a dress. (3) I explained it to Tom. (Indirect cannot precede); (4) I always speak English to her. (Indirect cannot precede); (5) Find him a good book. (6) Please pronounce these words for her/him. (Indirect cannot precede); (7) I made him a hotel reservation. (8) I sold him my old car. (9) Johnny closed the door for her/him. (Indirect cannot precede); (10) I lent him some money. (11) Please keep this money for her. (Indirect cannot precede); (12) I answered the question for him. (Indirect cannot precede); (13) He told him/her his story. (14) Please remember me to her. (Indirect cannot precede); (15) I introduced Mary to him. (Indirect cannot precede)

(Exercise 62.3)
(2) They repeated to the police the robbery... (3) He ordered me a ham and cheese sandwich... (4) They ordered sandwiches for the happy children... (5) Mary Wilson bought bathrobes for her husband and two sons. (6) Mrs. Avon bought her husband a new red wool bathrobe which was on sale. (7) John built for his parents a beautiful... (8)...Gordon Frakes gave $50,000 to the school. (9)...I've sent an old friend most of my...

(Exercise 62.4)
A: (1) Some money was offered to the city. (2) A story will be read to the children. (3) Some things were sold to the government. (4) Some money was given to the hospital. (5) Some pictures will be given to his friends. (6) A letter was shown to the president. (7) The problem was explained to them.
B: (2) She was taught English. (3) You will be given directions for getting here. (4) He will be offered a loan. (5) They had been given shots. (6) He has not yet been told the results of his examination.

(Exercise 63.1)
These sample answers use only one of many possible subjects. (3) Yes, her mother asked her to. (4) Yes, his boss wants him to. (5) Yes, the school requires him to. (6) Yes, the policeman ordered him to. (7) Yes, I would like her to.

(Exercise 64.1)
(3) We watched Bob go. (4) We made Bob go. (5) We ordered Bob to go. (6) We heard Bob go. (7) We asked Bob to go. (8) We told Bob to go. (9) We had Bob go. (10) We permitted Bob to go. (11) We saw Bob go. (12) We expected Bob to go.

SECTION 16

(Exercise 65.1)
(5) He remembers my asking. (6) He remembers their teaching him to swim. (7) He remembers taking his first trip. (8) He remembers his giving him a penny. (9) He remembers running away from home. (10) He remembers her giving him a haircut. (11) He remembers his/her keeping him after school. (12) He remembers losing all his money. (13) He remembers our giving him a bicycle. (14) He remembers playing in the park. (15) He remembers their taking him to the farm. (16) He remembers earning his first dollar. (17) He remembers our taking him to his first movie. (18) He remembers her teaching him how to dance. (19) He remembers fighting with his brother. (20) He remembers my taking his picture.

(Exercise 65.2)
These are possible questions and answers for this exercise.
2. Speaker A: What is Miss Dent concerned about?
   Speaker B: She's concerned about her son's getting failing grades (or failing all his subjects, or getting F's in all his subjects, or doing so poorly in school)
3. Speaker A: What does Ted remember?
   Speaker B: He remembers his Uncle John's bringing presents at Christmastime (or coming to visit)
4. Speaker A: What does Mrs. Dent resent?
   Speaker B: She resents her son's coming late to dinner (meals) all the time.
5. Speaker A: What is Susie laughing at?
   Speaker B: She's laughing at Johnny's falling down (or slipping on the ice.)
6. Speaker A: What does Mrs. Long depend on?
   Speaker B: She depends on Johnny's carrying the groceries for her.

(Exercise 68.2)
(4) I disliked Jean's calling. (5) I advised Jean to call. (6) I told Jean to call. (7) I made Jean call. (8) I felt eager for Jean to call. (9) I was tired of Jean's calling. (10) I enjoyed Jean's calling. (11) I looked forward to Jean's calling. (12) I let Jean call. (13) I expected Jean to call. (14) I was afraid for Jean to call. (15) I forgot about Jean's calling. (16) I watched Jean call. (17) I recommended Jean's calling. (18) I was delighted for Jean to call. (19) I waited for Jean to call. (20) I laughed about Jean's calling.

(Exercise 68.3)
(1) to come; (2) to apply; (3) shut; (4) make; (5) coming; (6) to tell; (7) to join; (8) getting; (9) disappear; (10) to stop; (11) to help; (12) playing; (13) make; (14) leaving; (15) write

English as a Second Language

Helen Brennan Memorial Library

English as a Second Language

Helen Brennan Memorial Library